CU00923093

BA
+ SOACHIM

Violin
Master Works &
Their Interpretation

G. MAILLARD KESSLERE B P

Violin
Master Works & Their Interpretation

LEOPOLD AUER

WITH A FOREWORD BY
Frederick H. Martens

Dover Publications, Inc.
Mineola, New York
1925

Bibliographical Note

This Dover edition, first published in 2012, is an unabridged republication of the work originally published in 1925 by Carl Fischer, Inc., New York.

Library of Congress Cataloging-in-Publication Data

Auer, Leopold, 1845-1930.
    Violin master works and their interpretation / Leopold Auer ; foreword by Fredrick H. Martens.
        p. cm.
    "This Dover edition, first published in 2012, is an unabridged republication of the work originally published in 1925 by Carl Fischer, Inc., New York."
    ISBN-13: 978-0-486-49911-6
    ISBN-10: 0-486-49911-1
    1. Violin music—Analysis, appreciation. I. Title.

MT140.A85 2012
787.2—dc23

2012014000

Manufactured in the United States by Courier Corporation
49911102
www.doverpublications.com

FOREWORD.

For the violinist—as for every musical artist—"interpretation," the living soul of playing, is the touchstone of his art. When he can translate in tone the thought, the spirit, the beauty of the music he plays so that it is revealed to his auditors with the clarity and beauty its composer intended, he is truly an interpreting artist."

The formulating of the "how" of interpretation, even with regard to those masterworks of the violin which every advanced student must know, is not so easy. As the author of this volume points out in his "Introduction," the student himself must be equipped with a very definite quota of technique, musical intuition and good taste before he can hope to derive major benefit from the detailed interpretative consideration of any important work.

It may safely be said that there are only a few individual figures in the violin world whose outstanding achievement and authority would secure for their views that general respect which would make such consideration valid. For the interpretation of a musical composition always remains to such a degree an individual and personal matter, that only the utterances of an interpreter whose experience and authority were unquestioned would secure for his conclusions the practical acknowledgement which would make them most widely useful and beneficial.

That the aesthetic and practical views of the man who has formed that brilliant galaxy of contemporary violin virtuosos known as the "Russian school," anent the interpretation of the master works of the violin are invaluable to every student of the instrument may be taken for granted. And yet, with the instinctive modesty common to those whose achievement is real, Professor Auer at first hesitated to commit himself to a book on a subject which so greatly interested him and which he was so uniquely fitted to consider.

The writer, with whom Professor Auer discussed the matter when the subject of the present volume was mooted, was instrumental in overcoming his first hesitation and this may have led Professor Auer to suggest his "Foreword" for a

III

volume which proves how adequately its author has handled his delicate and elusive subject. It was a request with which the writer was happy to comply, since it has given him an opportunity of outlining the work's outstanding qualities.

Some will be so self-evident to the student that they do not call for extended consideration. It is at once clear that the author is modest. He brings no tablets from the Mount. He presents his own opinions with respect and tolerance for those of others. He is neither an individualist nor a traditionalist, but renders unto artistic individuality and tradition that which is due to each.

Then, too, the plan of the work is elastic. From the great body of violin literature Professor Auer has chosen for detailed interpretative analysis and discussion some seventy odd major compositions; in practically every case "living" works, compositions which form a vital part of the existing violin repertoire. They follow each other in an informal chronological sequence and, though he is careful to establish the character of the individual work and of its period, the author has eschewed extended biographical or other digressions not bearing on the subject. "After all," he remarked to the writer, "there are enough good biographical dictionaries and individual biographies to which any student may refer. I feel that my book will be practically useful in direct proportion to the fullness of detail with which it considers its subject—the interpretation of the masterworks written for the violin."

And with due regard for the personal equation in interpretation, which Professor Auer never forgets, he has concentrated on analyzing the masterworks of violin literature in clear, practical expositions of how each should be played in order to do justice to the work and to the player. Noteworthy are the invaluable hints and directions regarding the technical *minutiæ* of interpretation: special bowings; mood and tempo variants; artistic effects; methods of individual procedure which Professor Auer uses with his own pupils; individual "cuts" which enhance the audition of a work on the recital stage, etc., all drawn from the author's rich fund of artistic experience. And in many cases the author supports his interpretative views by citing the actual opinions and procedure of such composers and artists as Joachim, Vieuxtemps, Wieniawski, Saint-Saëns, Wilhelmj, Sarasate, Sivori and others, whom he heard play most of the works to be considered and with whom he discussed them.

A large number of musical examples, covering all the detail of the author's interpretative directions make the niceties of tempo, dynamics, special bowings, fingerings, etc., clear to the student beyond any manner of doubt; and as a pendant to the more important individual works considered, a concluding chapter develops the author's ideas with regard to "Transcriptions" and "Musical Memory," two subjects intimately linked with his theme; the first with the repertoire, the second with its presentation.

The present volume is the third which its author has written. From the point of view of the student it is, perhaps, the most valuable. The values of the delightful "My Long Life in Music," in which Professor Auer has told the story of one of the most interesting of musical careers, are more purely literary and cultural. "Violin Playing as I Teach It" is devoted to the fundamental practical and aesthetic aspects of the art. But the "Violin Master Works and Their Interpretation" might be called the authoritative text-book of a master on interpretation whose teachings and influence have been revealed by pupils and interpreters such as Elman, Heifetz, Zimbalist and a score of others. And there can be no question but that the student who "marks, learns and inwardly digests it" will realize its author's hope that he will "find himself better able to express the soul, the thought, the spirit of the great creators of all that is finest in violin music."

FREDERICK H. MARTENS.

INTRODUCTION.

To express the inexplicable so that it can be understood, to define and segregate the experiences and reactions of musical emotion so that they may be grasped by the invisible eye of the spirit, is not easy. My aim is to offer the young violinist and student a legacy, a tangible evidence of my long years of experience as an interpreting artist and a teacher of the classic literature of the violin, with regard to the interpretation of the great works of the ancient as well as the modern masters.

In my opinion the question of musical style is one that can be considered only from a purely individual standpoint: it is not possible to determine *exactly* how the Beethoven Concerto or the Bach Chaconne should be played. A hundred years ago and two hundred years ago people played, and heard with other ears than those of our own twentieth century, the age of the telephone and the radio. Our nervous system is a more irritable one than that of our great-grandfathers yet, though I am not a blind follower of tradition, there are certain principles of musical aesthetics which remain authoritative with regard to the interpretation of the classic masterpieces.

The artist who unconsciously acknowledges and possesses these principles, provided he also commands the technique necessary to control all mechanical difficulties, will cause the work he is playing to impress the listener as it was meant to do. He will make his auditor feel its content in accordance with the intention of its creator. I always have found, even in the most provincial Russian cities, that any notable composition, when played in the proper manner, made a profound impression on the musically most uncultivated listener: he reacted to this impression, even though quite unconsciously.

When we take an audience of several thousand persons gathered on some important occasion at Carnegie Hall, New York, or in one of the larger European concert halls, we are obliged to admit that a large proportion of these auditors, probably, are not musically educated. Yet how different are the impressions made on the audience as a whole by two different orchestral conductors or two different virtuosos, each presenting the same work! One conductor—and, strictly speaking, a conductor, too, is first of all a virtuoso—or instrumental virtuoso will rouse an audience to enthusiasm by his presentation of a certain work; while another, playing the self-same composition, will leave them quite cold; and yet, both may be absolutely competent, technically speaking. Is this because in the second instance the conductor or player presents the work along the lines laid down by tradition, while in the first case the artist seeks to express the composer's meaning through the medium of his own feelings, his own emotions? I believe this last to be true. I believe in talent, in genius, in sensitive reaction to the beautiful, in aesthetic sensibility—for aesthetic sensibility is the law of the beautiful—and not in tradition.

When I was a young man Joachim was accounted the greatest interpreter of the Beethoven Violin Concerto, Bach's Chaconne, and Tartini's sonata "The Devil's Trill." Whenever and wherever Joachim played for the first time one of these works was listed on his programme. Does this mean to imply that Vieuxtemps, Wieniawski or Wilhelmj did not play the same works just as well? The three violinists last mentioned were also great artists, endowed with a perfected technique. Vieuxtemps and Wieniawski were also distinguished violin composers; while Wilhelmj, perhaps, possessed the largest and most evenly beautiful violin tone of his time and yet. . . .

It is true that Joachim never played compositions by Vieuxtemps or Wieniawski, nor did he play Bach's "Air on the G String" in the transcription which Wilhelmj has made so popular. In this particular field Joachim either could not or would not compete with his colleagues aforementioned though they, as distinguished virtuosos, also included the classic repertoire in their programmes. This proves that Joachim possessed the true feeling and perception, the right sense of style where Bach, Beethoven and the older Italian composers were concerned. He made a deep impression on his auditors; and he amply gratified their sense of beauty when he played the works of these masters and those of Schumann, Spohr and Viotti. Later he included the masterly transcriptions he had made of the Brahms' "Hungarian Dances," (originally composed for the piano, four-hands) in his repertoire since, himself by birth a Hungarian, these dances were dear to his heart. It is seldom, in the course of the past twenty years, that I have heard other artists play these dances "in character," and in the manner that this uniquely original music demands. In most cases the rapid tempos are hurried, the slow movements are dragged, the *ritenuti* as well as the *accellerandi* are exaggerated, owing to which the rhythm suffers. And rhythm is the foundation of all music and of Hungarian music in particular.

There are only a few of the elect who are able to correctly grasp the character of the music which they interpret; who divine the composer's intention, who know how to make a distinction between lyric and dramatic music, to differentiate a heroic from a tender theme, to separate the supervirile urge which thrills a moment of passion from the jocose or the gracious mood in their interpretation. Only a few are able to spread out the rich color-shadings of tone as the inspired painter does on his palette before transfering them to his canvas. Monotony, colorlessness, lack of shading will destroy the beauty of the finest work. I tell my pupils, again and again, that every single dynamic sign or accent mark with which the composer or an authoritative editor has provided a composition, is every bit as important as the note it qualifies. Unfortunately, most students and often even matured musicians and solo artists are content to play the notes without regard for the above mentioned considerations. And there also is another type of monotony which creeps into the performance of outstanding works: this is the monotony of tempos. Only a few composers possess the gift of setting down their meaning clearly and exactly on paper. This is, in truth, extremely difficult and in most cases almost impossible, though Beethoven forms an exception to this rule. The performance of his chamber music, in particular, demands a wealth of hitherto unsuspected individual shadings which are purely Beethovenian. In such works the interpreter's talent, his temperament, his appreciation of beauty and his delicacy of perception for the intimate character of the various themes is revealed. They also throw into relief that inexplicable something, so highly important to the musical ear—the *variation* of tempos in one and the same composition. Whether it be a concerto, a romance, a scherzo or a nocturne, the principle remains the same. Only in the delicate and absolutely unobtrusive application of this principle does a distinction exist.

Since this principle of the *variation* of tempo and shading is the life-principle of any composition played, since it reveals the soul of the composer's music, it underlies the interpretation of every important work in violin literature, classic as well as modern.

In dealing with the interpretation of the masterworks of the violin repertoire, my one great object has been to supply the serious student with hints and suggestions based on my own experience and practice, and on that of some of the greatest interpreting artists of the instrument the world has known, artists who were the contemporaries of my younger days, and anent whose ideas of style and interpretation I can speak from actual knowledge and observation.

The observations, hints and suggestions which I have to offer are not put forward as ironclad rules, as uncontrovertible laws. While they endeavor to determine the rightful values of *nuance* and shading in the playing of the great repertoire works they are often tentative—one must always remember that in many compositions, in many individual passages the aesthetic sense permits of conceptions which may differ, and which in spite of the fact are justified by the best canons of musical and artistic good taste. Yet in general, especially in the case of certain outstanding works, the work itself, its character, is so clear that irrespective of variations in detail presentation the interpretation, broadly speaking, must follow certain obvious lines of development.

I have tried in every case, where a detail of interpretation might be open to question, to give reasons which have prompted my own idea of how it should be handled, with due regard for the validity of other and dissenting opinions.

As I already have stated musical style and interpretation can be considered only from a purely individual standpoint. Yet without losing sight of this fact, or that tradition is all too often only the dead letter of the law of musical beauty and not its living spirit, there remains much to be said which should be of direct and practical benefit to the student anxious to express in his playing the true inwardness of the great repertoire works. In the following pages I have tried to give the student a better insight into the meaning, the expressive content of the Violin Master Works. Should they help him to express more perfectly the soul, the thought, the spirit of the creators of all that is finest in violin music, I shall be well content.

The Author.

CONTENTS

CONTENTS—Continued

CONTENTS—Continued

Chapter I

OUTSTANDING WORKS OF THE OLDER ITALIAN VIOLIN COMPOSERS.

With regard to the older Italian composers it might be said that during the last decades of the nineteenth and the first of the twentieth century, many of their compositions, written in the seventeenth and eighteenth centuries, have been "discovered" in various German and Italian libraries by treasure-seekers duly qualified (or the reverse), and have been edited and published by them. Among these works, now and again, we find one by some more important older Italian composer, works which for all they may not be on quite the level of those already known to us, closely approximate them in musical value.

The great majority of these exhumed compositions with which the market has been flooded, however, are decidedly uninteresting, monotonous and dry as regards invention, and once more prove that even celebrated masters cannot turn out sonatas by the hundred with impunity. Still less are their unworthy imitators able to do so; real, genuine music is something which must be experienced, felt, divined—and then created! It can be imitated only as regards its externals.

Even geniuses like Corelli, Veracini and Giuseppe Tartini, upon whom Veracini exercised so great an influence, are not free from this reproach of overproduction at the expense of quality, and it must be confessed that the reissue of such compositions often seems to have no other justification than the mistaken piety of the discoverer or a purely commercial reason.

I cannot help feeling that when in their own day such masters as Mendelssohn and Ferdinand David, after a thorough examination of the manuscripts to be found in the state libraries of Berlin, Dresden and Leipsic, completed their selection, they made generally available all that was most important, all that deserved wider recognition. None among the works *discovered* (?) toward the end of the past or at the beginning of the present century compare as regards imaginative and creative importance with such works as Tartini's two sonatas in G minor (including the "Devil's Trill"

1

Sonata); Corelli's "Follia d'Espagna"; the two Sonatas by Locatelli edited by Julius Röntgen, in Amsterdam; the D major Sonata and E minor Concerto by Nardini; and Vitali's "Ciaconna."*

In the works just mentioned we find, aside from musical invention, dramatic conception and perfection of form. They rank among the most significant compositions included in the entire range of violin literature, And their spontaneity is not merely a mental, an intellectual originality, an originality of clever calculation, as is the case with the majority of newly-discovered works by distinguished masters, whose very names are full of promise; but they have their origin in those deep founts from which genius alone draws inspiration.

Tartini's "Devil's Trill" Sonata ** (*Il Trillo del Diavolo*) —Tartini was a bit of a mystic—came to him in a dream,*** and if it really was inspired by the devil, proves that whatever his other faults, His Satanic Majesty is a musician of the first order.

The First Movement of the "Devil's Trill" Sonata, a *Larghetto affetuoso*, begins in lyric style, yet ever and anon takes a profoundly sorrowful inflection as, for instance, in the fourth measure after letter A:

---

* Revised and edited by Leopold Auer. Carl Fischer, Inc., New York.

** Giuseppe Tartini, Sonata (Il Trillo del Diavolo). Revised and edited by Leopold Auer. Carl Fischer, Inc., New York.

*** Tartini's own verbal account of how he came to write it (Laland: *Voyage d'un François en Italie, en 1765 et 1766, Tome 8)*, is worth quoting, since it may aid the student to fix the mood of the whole composition. Says the composer: "One night, it was in the year 1713, I dreamed that I had signed over my soul to the devil. All went exactly according to my desire, and my new servant anticipated my every wish. It occurred to me, among other things, to hand him my violin in order to see whether he would be able to play some of the tones I heard in my dream. How great was my astonishment, however, when I heard a sonata so glorious and beautiful, and played with so great an art and understanding that it seemed beyond the most daring flight of human fancy! I was carried away, delighted and enraptured to such a degree that I could hardly breathe, and I awoke! At once I seized my violin in order to catch and hold at least some of the tones I heard in my dream. In vain. It is true that the music I composed on this occasion is the best I ever wrote in my life, and I still call it 'The Devil's Sonata;' yet the gulf between it and that which had so moved me is so great that I would have broken my instrument and foresworn music forever, had I found it possible to deprive myself of the enjoyment it gives me."

and where the same phrase is repeated a third lower:

at the end of the first movement, which closes very quietly on a long trill. I should like to mention that *Larghetto* is not synonomous with *Largo;* in other words, the movement should not be dragged as it sometimes is when heard on the concert platform, since dragging detracts from its effect.

The Second Movement, in contrast to its predecessor, begins very energetically and is followed by short, ironic little trills— I say "short" because care must be taken that they are not extended so that their length interferes with the *flow* of the melody. I advise my pupils *not* to put the rhythmic accent on the trill *itself*, but to make it *after* the trill, that is, to stress the note on which the trill is based, as for example:

Expression marks and dynamic signs must be strictly observed if the movement is to produce the desired effect.

The *Grave* which follows (Third Movement) had best be taken in 8/8 time, that is to say, with great breadth. It leads over into the *Allegro assai* in 2/4 time, which contains the "Devil's Trill." The latter begins very *piano* and by means of a tremendous *crescendo* leads over into the *Grave* (played as before) which follows, with the difference that this time the latter occurs on the dominant, in D minor. In order to secure the greatest clearness and rhythmic pregnancy I advise the following rhythmic division of the trill-sequence:

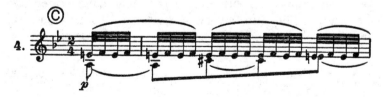

After a repetition of the *Grave* and the *Allegro assai*, this time on the tonic, we have the Cadenza, which is founded on the Initial Theme of the Sonata, the *Larghetto*, and should be played in that tempo. Then, after a chain of trills, very broadly played, we have an allusion to the preceding *Allegro*, and the composition ends with a long, preparatory *ritenuto* and a tremendous working-up of tone that carries us to the final *Adagio*.

It stands to reason that Tartini must have composed a large number of sonatas (as a matter of fact his published compositions alone include some forty sonatas and eighteen concertos) when we consider that both his two best-known and most deservedly popular works—the "Devil's Trill" Sonata and the Sonata in G minor—are written in the same key. The Sonata in G minor* goes beyond Corelli and Vivaldi as regards development of form and musical content. Tartini is said to have been in the habit of reading one of Petrarch's sonnets before beginning to compose, and in view of the poetic beauty of the Sonata in G minor one is inclined to think he hit upon an especially fine sonnet by the Italian poet before he wrote this work.

The First Movement, *Adagio*, in 8/8 time, demands a warm, lovely quality of tone in order adequately to convey the sorrowful character of its music, whose plaintiveness is notably emphasized in the second measure from the beginning by the use of the augmented second E flat and F sharp. This mood dominates the entire sonata, although now and again a modulation leading into B flat establishes a mood more quiet and consolatory. I must here repeat that quite aside from the beauty inherent in this music itself, it calls for the needful variations of tonal color in order to express the details of that

---

* In Tartini's own day this sonata was called *Didone abbandonata* ("Dido the Forsaken"). My observations refer to the edition I have published, revised and edited for the firm of Carl Fischer, Inc., New York.

beauty. For instance, in the second measure after letter **C**:

the greatest serenity and equality is demanded while playing the eight sixteenth notes, which repeat through several measures and move to the climax:

in a continuous *piano* with a preceding working-up of the tonal volume. Five measures before the end of the movement we have a similar passage which, however, ends with a *piano*.

A passionate and tempestuous urgency rages throughout the entire second movement of the sonata, the *Non troppo presto*. Here too, in most cases, the observance of the accents which fall on the majority of the notes beginning the measure with a mordent:

and also at letter **A**:

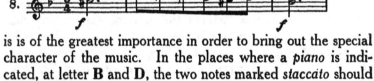

is is of the greatest importance in order to bring out the special character of the music. In the places where a *piano* is indicated, at letter **B** and **D**, the two notes marked *staccato* should be played as "flying" *staccati* with a light bow. The concluding five measures, marked *Più lento*, should be taken very broadly, the trill:

should be decidedly long sustained, and the final note played strongly, *without any diminuendo!*

The third movement, *Largo*, must be played with great breadth, as an introduction to the *Allegro commodo*, and the *Allegro commodo* itself should be taken in a tempo approximating a *Moderato*. I am not of the opinion that this movement should be played in too slow a tempo; the tempo is very exactly indicated and in view of this fact (i.e., that too broad and extended a tempo is uncalled for) at letter **C**:

10.

p leggiero

I have marked the eighth-notes with a *leggiero* in order to avoid monotony in phrasing. The second part of the movement begins with the same light *spiccato* and, in part, *staccato* bowings:

11.

p

for the reason already given. All the other notes are to be taken with a *détaché* stroke, and the whole movement should be played with a somewhat melancholy tonal color. The *Più lenti* in the second and in the last movement should be observed only when indicated, and then only the second time, that is, when the section in question is repeated.

Archangelo Corelli (1853-1713) whose contemporaries called him "Prince of Music" and "Master of Masters," aside from his *Concerti grossi* wrote some sixty sonatas; and his compositions, though centuries have passed, still remain classics. From the standpoint of the violin repertoire of the present day, the sixth sonata of his group of *Sonate a Violino e Violone o Cembalo* (Rome, 1700) cannot be overlooked. For the fifth movement of this sonata is the famous "Follia" with sixteen variations.

The "Follia" or "Folies d'Espagne": this group of violin variations with figured bass is one of the most important of the works of the old Italian school. As a "modern" repertoire number it has existed since Ferdinand David edited it after the original edition with a very adequate piano accompaniment. Since then it often has been included in the recital programmes of the greatest virtuosos as well as used in the studios of most teachers, by whom it is regarded as essential study material for the aspiring violinist.

The numerous variations of the Corelli "Follia" are in some sort a compilation of the technical problems of bowing and at the same time supply highly instructive left-hand studies. In my own edition* I have not touched the piano accompaniment, but only have indicated changes in the solo violin part where such changes seemed necessary.

The first and main essential in making this composition enjoyable to the musician as well as to the layman, is the *exact* observation of the changes of tempo in the different variations. We already have to contend with the monotony due to the fact that the "Follia" is written in one key, the key of D minor, from beginning to end, without a change. If to this we add monotony of movement and, perhaps, do not vary our tone, then the composition is bound to make a tiring impression, even though it may be played technically in an impeccable manner.

Its theme unquestionably gives this serious work its character of high meaning and importance. As Corelli uses it the phrase "Folies d'Espagne" is equivalent to "Scenes of Madness."† It calls for warm expressive interpretation, both when first played, *forte*, and when repeated *pianissimo*.

At letter **B** play tempestuously:

12.

* Archangelo Corelli, "Les Folies d'Espagne." Revised and edited by Leopold Auer. Carl Fischer, Inc., New York.

† Originally the "Folia" was an old fourteenth century Spanish dance, danced to the accompaniment of flutes and castagnettes, and its title, seeing that it is a very lively and vivacious dance, suggests the "madness" of pleasure rather than insanity. The more sinister meaning may have developed out of an historical association. Don Pedro I, King of Portugal, was passionately fond of the "Folia" when a young prince. He would spend whole nights dancing it with his beautiful mistress Inez de Castro (d. 1355) by candlelight in the palace of Coimbra. But the Castro family was hated by the Portuguese nobles, and Inez was stabbed to death in the presence of Pedro's father. When Pedro came to the throne he had Inez's assassins put to death amid terrible tortures and exhuming her body, forced the assembled nobles of Portugal to swear homage to the corpse as their queen, kissing her withered hand. Since that time the "Madness" (Folias) of the dance has been madness in the sinister sense Corelli's music represents.

making the *sforzandi* without forcing the tone. The variation
following, at letter **C**, should be taken *spiccato*, with a very
light wrist. At letter **E**:

the same bowing should be used. At letter **F** chords must
be played very shortly and energetically whenever they occur
in the variation. At letter **H**, on the other hand:

the student should play very expressively and should emphasize
his accents by means of left-hand vibration rather than the bow.

At letter **K** great animation is in order and at letter **L**:

the working-up from *piano* to *forte* should be strongly marked.
At letter **M**, *Adagio*, the student should count eight eighths
and make his violin sing. At letter **N**:

he must play quietly, and should not forget to accent the third
eighth of each measure. At letter **O**, in 12/8 time, the bow
must be cast very lightly on the strings and there should be no
firm *staccato* used. At letter **P**, *Adagio*, play with much ex-

pression, and at letter **Q** take the *Lento*, in 9/8 time, somewhat
more slowly than the preceding *Adagio*. At letter **R**:

the student should play in a light and animated manner as a
contrast to the two preceding variations. At letter **S** all details
are indicated with great exactness and it may be mentioned
that this variation is first and foremost a *technical* study. At
letter **V**, the tempo is the same as that of the variation preceding
it, yet toward its close it grows quieter and at **W**—*Meno mosso*
—it becomes slower. After letter **Y** comes the closing
Cadenza: the player should begin it very quietly, keep to this
mood during the long trill, and take the closing chord with
great breadth.

Antonio Vivaldi's (c. 1675-1743) Concerto in A minor*
is one of the best, if not the best and most frequently played of
the many concertos written by its prolific composer. Arranged
and published with string orchestra and organ accompaniment,
it has won acceptance in the concert hall because of its wealth
of melody and the variety of the tonal colors which orchestra
and organ weave about the solo violin.

In order to interpret this Concerto properly the player first
of all must have a feeling for musical style and a gift for rich
tone colors; an exact observance of the correct bowings and
of the dynamic signs will then follow as a matter of course.

The first movement is marked *Allegro*. To this *Allegro* I
should like to add a *moderato,* for if this be done we have the
tempo which is best suited to the somewhat melancholy character of this movement. The broad *détaché* stroke prescribed
in *forte* as well as in *piano* must be strictly observed, and the
martellato occasionally indicated for one or more measures on
the one hand gives the music its special character, and on the
other interrupts and varies the *détaché* bowing which dominates
throughout the movement.

---

* Arranged and edited by Tivadar Nachez. Carl Fischer, Inc., New York.

The *Largo*, unfortunately, is somewhat short; and hence its
tempo should be all the more deliberate.   It stands to reason,
therefore, that a division of the measure into eight-eighths be
observed in this movement, so that the sixteenth-notes represent-
ing the melody be produced as broadly and singingly as possible, which can only result in enhancing the charm of this
Largo. A most exquisite moment occurs at the measure marked
misterioso:

to be played mysteriously, as though holding the breath.   The
sole drawback to this movement is that it is not long enough;
it lasts so short a time.

In the concluding movement, the Presto, the bowings indicated by the editor, *détaché* and *martellato* give this Finale
its unique character.   In the middle of the movement occurs
the following passage:

which should be played very delicately and flowingly. Eight
measures before the close we have another passage:

which also should be taken very delicately to begin with, but
which, two measures before the end, should terminate with a
great broadening out of tone and a big *ritardando* on the *forte*
of the concluding notes.

The Ciaconna in G minor† by Tommasso Vitali, son of the
Cremonese violinist, Giovanni Battista Vitali, established in
Bologna in 1706, is a forerunner of Bach's great work in the

† Ciaconna in G minor, by Tommasso Vitali.   Revised and edited by Leopold
Auer, Carl Fischer, Inc., New York.

same form for violin solo. It is a "Ciaconna" with variations,
in which a clean-cut rhythmic theme is developed in a number
of contrasting variations whose ornamentation is no mere external, virtuoso embellishment, but forms part and parcel of
the working out of the Main Theme itself. The first eight
measures of the organ or piano introduction, which always
impress the listener by their combination of outward simplicity
and inner grandeur, establish the proper mood of the composition in the auditor's mind, and make him more susceptible to
what is to follow—the grandly laid out Theme with its interesting variations, which fascinate by reason of their musical
content, as well as because of their variety of technical figuration. A special charm of these variations is the change of
tonality which occurs in certain ones among them—something
unusual in seventeenth-century compositions—and some decidedly inspired modulations. I know no other work of its
period which compares with the Vitali "Ciaconna" as regards
wealth of harmonic development. This, however, may be due
in part to David who, when he edited the work for his "High
School of Violin Playing," in various instances departed
widely from his original. His transcription, however, is held
by the best authorities to represent a valid approximation of
Vivaldi's manner of writing.

Already, in the Third Variation, we find ourselves moving
in B flat minor, then in G flat major, D flat major, and all
the various keys related to the original key of G minor. On
a closer examination of the work we find that in it, as in Bach's
"Ciaconna," each variation has a clearly marked, individual
character of its own; and that this special character has been
intensified by Ferdinand David's organ or piano accompaniment in a masterly way, so that when the solo player is properly
supported by his accompanist the collective effect is greatly
heightened. The basic mood note of the "Ciaconna" is a
dramatic one: the observation of the slight changes of tempo
such as, in Variation Two: *Un poco più animato;* in Variation
Three: *Espressivo agitato;* in Variation Four: *Leggiero ed un
poco vivo,* is of quite particular importance, because these little
contrasts in tempo and movement, these slight modifications in
mood, emphasize the fundamental character of the entire work.

Four measures before Variation Six we have an *a tempo:*

21.

to be played "sighingly," the eighth-notes quite short, produced
to sound like a catching of the breath.   In variation Six, again,
we move to a *Più largo* and "sing."   Variation Eight should
be played with great breadth.   This variation leads over to
the theme, *Tempo primo, fortissimo.*   As it does so in A minor
and at quite some length, it becomes monotonous.   For this
reason I have indicated a little "cut," from Variation Nine
to Variation Ten.   One of the "Ciaconna's" loveliest moments
is in Variation Eleven, *pp, dolcissimo:*

22.

that is to say, it should be played so that it is hardly audible.
It should sound as though played in the far distance, the bow
lying on the strings without the faintest pressure from the wrist,
while the left hand carries out a sustained *vibrato.*

The sustained *vibrato* is against my principles, and in general
I teach only a moderate *vibrato,* and then only on sustained
notes.   The above case, however, represents an exception to
the rule.   After a *Crescendo poco a poco,* we have Variation
Twelve, also presented *pp,* notwithstanding which its beautiful melody should be played with the most tender warmth and
intimacy.

Variation Thirteen has a four-measure stretto which leads
suddenly over into a *Piano espressivo,* and with Variation
Fourteen the great working-up begins with an *Un poco vivo,*
marked *sempre pianissimo:*

23.

which leads to the climax, the theme, *ff*, and the *Largamente* in the fundamental key of G minor.

Variation Fifteen, which follows, is of a pronounced passionate character, the only one of its kind in the entire composition:

and the mood endures until Variation Sixteen, which is played with far greater breadth of tempo and with majestic serenity. Variation Seventeen urges on its triplets in a constantly increasing *Più vivo* up to Variation Eighteen, where the tempo gradually becomes quieter until the *Più largo:*

is reached

Variation Nineteen at:

introduces the most difficult passage in the composition with regard to tone-production. From this point on there begins, with the softest possible tone, a sustained *crescendo* twelve measures long, played in a slow tempo by both instruments, the violin and the piano or organ. Little by little it increases in volume of tone until the climaxing point at the *fortissimo* is reached. Then the theme once more appears and the work concludes with a tremendous *rallentando*, and a Cadenza on the long-sustained *fff* double trill.

Pietro Locatelli (1693-1764), Corelli's pupil, is remembered not so much because of his "L'Arte del Violino," which in addition to twelve concertos contains the "24 Caprices" from which Paganini drew suggestions for those he himself wrote, but principally owing to two fine sonatas which still form part of the concert repertoire of his instrument.

The Sonata in G major* by Locatelli is one of the few eighteenth-century violin sonatas which exist in only one edition. Ferdinand David's collection, "The High School of Violin Playing," contains a Sonata in G minor, by Locatelli, it is true; yet it is entirely different from the one in G major, not alone in key but in character as well. The first of these two Locatelli Sonatas with which we are concerned comprises four movements: *Largo, Allegro, Andante* and *Allegro.* Quite contrary to the custom of Locatelli's day, which demanded that all the movements of a sonata be written in the same key, in this work the two slow movements are in G minor, and the two Allegros in G major, and this gives the whole composition a quality of life and color in decided contrast to other sonatas of the same period.

The *Largo* has an imposing theme whose majestic character is emphasized by the two General Pauses at the end of the first measure:

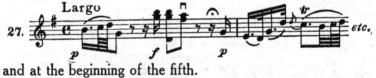

and at the beginning of the fifth.

The last mentioned hold being conceived as an echo. As in the slow movements of other of these older Italian works the student should divide his four quarter-notes into eight eighth-notes.

The succeeding *Allegro* is conceived as a movement very energetic in character and, thanks to the variety of bowings and their shading, it is very colorful. These *nuances* of stroke

---

* Pietro Locatelli. Sonata in G major. Revised and edited with piano accompaniment by Julius Röntgen. G. Alsbach & Co., Amsterdam.

and bow-inflection must be exactly carried out if the movement is to produce the proper effect.

The *Andante* might be termed a *"Siciliano,"* for it has all the melodic charm and the melancholy of mood peculiar to the old art-dance known by that name. A passage which reveals these qualities in a characteristic manner is the following one:

29.

f molto espressivo

which should be played with sorrowful expression.

The concluding *Allegro* is probably the most noteworthy of the four movements. In it both composer and editor have done their best. The composer has supplied a fresh, animated theme which contains an alternating four-quarter and three-quarter rhythm that is continued through the entire compoistion; a procedure which was a novelty two hundred years ago, and which even now lends the piece a stamp of entire independence. The editor, as his share, has provided the spontaneous theme of the first four measures with a corresponding counterpoint in the upper voice of the piano part, which clarifies and illumines the whole in a musically most grateful manner.

Allegro
detaché

30.

(5th measure)

The movement ends with a Cadenza by the editor to whom credit is also due for having provided the whole Sonata with highly expressive and musical *nuances* and shadings.

The Sonata in F minor,* the second of the Locatelli Sonatas here considered, is especially interesting because its most notable

---

* Pietro Locatelli. Sonata in F minor. Revised and edited with piano accompaniment by Julius Röntgen. G. Alsbach & Co., Amsterdam.

characteristic is the composer's evident attempt to blaze new trails in the traditional sonata form customary in his day. There is an Introduction, and then comes a *Largo* with three *Grave*, around which are woven various little Cadenzas and which together form the First Movement. These Cadenzas apparently were written by the composer himself, and I judge that this is the case because in their shaping up they in no way or manner reflect more modern technical acquisitions. Besides, in another edition of this Sonata in F minor, edited by the late Miss Maud Powell (G. Schirmer, Inc., New York), these same Cadenzas are identical with those in the Röntgen edition.

The Second Movement is a *Vivace, ma non troppo*, and the third an "Aria con variazioni sul basso con ostinato," which the editor has provided with a concluding Cadenza. The customary final movement is lacking, and in spite of its melodic richness and beauty this Sonata does not escape a certain monotony due to the use of the key of F minor throughout, and the want of contrasting moods in its three movements.

The First Movement, *Largo*, is short and serves to introduce the first *Grave*, with the following theme:

After the first Cadenza comes the second *Grave*, a *Non troppo lento*, which forms the second section of the Theme. Then, following an interruption in the form of a second Cadenza, the Theme appears as the third *Grave* (again *Non troppo lento*), and the movement ends with the third Cadenza.

The Second Movement, *Vivace non troppo:*

introduces a little life and change in contrast to the preceding and the succeeding slow movement, and the more energetically and vigorously the student plays it the better effect it will make.

The "Aria con variazioni" on a ground bass *(basso ostinato)* with which the Sonata in F minor concludes, is one of the loveliest inspirations of the period in which it was written. A note of the deepest, sincerest anguish is voiced by the Theme, especially in the second section:

And in this theme the key of F minor makes a grateful and welcome impression.

In the Third Variation, *Poco più moto:*

the impression made on the listener is due entirely to the harmonious blending of the two expressive voices moving together.

The Fifth Variation, provided with the indications *Appassionato, forte* and *con gran' espressione,* is charmingly thrown into relief by a brilliant figuration for the left hand in the piano accompaniment. The closing Cadenza, conforming to the original in style, has been supplied by the editor.

Pietro Nardini (1722-1793), together with his teacher Tartini and Locatelli, is one of the most important composers of the post-Corellian epoch. His Sonata in D major* as well as his violin Concerto in E minor are among the most beautiful works of their day, works to whose musical and artistic values is added their usefulness as study material.

The *Adagio* at the beginning of the first movement calls for a very deliberate playing of the eighth-notes as in similar movements by Bach, Handel and the Italian masters of the seventeenth and eighteenth centuries. The *Allegro* which follows is accompanied by the phrase *con fuoco:* This explanatory phrase added by the composer is one which I most whole-heartedly endorse. The movement is an exceptionally

---

* Pietro Nardini, Sonata in D major. Revised and edited by Theodore Spiering. Carl Fischer, Inc., New York.

long one, and unless it be played with animated and fiery expressiveness and with the most exact observance of all interpretative and dynamic indications it would weary the listener.

The third movement, *Larghetto*, is an aria meant to be sung on the violin. In addition the composer has written *non tardante, semplice e mezza voce*. I advise every student when he reads these indications set down by the composer to turn to them in the pages of a good dictionary of musical terms in order to recall their exact meaning to memory.

The succeeding *Allegretto grazioso (Assai vivace)* brings up a point for consideration in connection with the turn indicated for the second note at the beginning of the theme. This turn gives the latter a somewhat clumsy character and I believe that two grace notes, as indicated in the following illustration, would be more in keeping with the composer's intentions:

35.

The movement is technically not hard to overcome; but it demands strongly developed fingers in the left hand and a *light* bow-stroke: a short *staccato* from the wrist for the two eighth-notes in the *piano* would be what the French express in the word *picquer*. The two grace notes may also be used at the letter **L**:

36.

and at similar points. At letter **N** play as at the beginning of the *Allegretto grazioso*.

One of the loveliest of all eighteenth century violin concertos is Pietro Nardini's Concerto in E minor* which, owing to the artistic good taste of its talented author, still graces many a concert programme of the present day. It starts with a very

---

* Pietro Nardini. Concerto in E minor. Concert Arrangement by Miska Hauser.
Carl Fischer, Inc., New York.

energetic theme of four measures, after which there is a change of mood, and the animated beginning is succeeded by a sorrow-freighted melody:

37.

These contrasts are repeated throughout the first movement, and the student should pay special attention to this alternation of mood to bring out the "light" and "dark" colors in their respective places. Here the first condition essential to proper interpretation, aside from musical sensibility, is an exact observation of the dynamic and other signs prescribed. With regard to the second movement, the "Andante Cantabile," its beauty is decidedly enhanced if it be played *con sordino.* The third movement is an *Allegretto Giocoso.* A happy development in the invention of the First Theme of this last movement is the change from minor to major and *vice versa* in the initial measures and, later, at the beginning of the second section. The Cadenza:

38.

should be taken very rhythmically, and without any change of tempo, and I would advise the student to play the concluding passage (changed as follows):

39.

in the manner above indicated—*not Spiccato!*—and with marked accentuation of the two chords.

CHAPTER II.

BACH'S CONTRIBUTION TO THE VIOLIN REPERTOIRE.

In writing anent instrumental music of any kind we must hark back with devotion to its originator, its real creator, Johann Sebastian Bach (1685-1750), the source and fountainhead of all music to the present day, whose genius influenced most of the greater composers who followed him at a later date* and helped develop their own genius.

The history of music tells the tale of Felix Mendelssohn's discovery of the great Bach choral compositions, and of that epoch-making performance of the "St. Matthews' Passion" in Berlin, in 1829, which first called general attention to the unique value and importance of Bach's creative work. And it was Ferdinand David in Leipzic who earned the undying gratitude of the violinistic world by discovering the "Solo Sonatas for Violin" and the famous "Six Sonatas for Violin and Piano." David edited and published these works, and Joseph Joachim was the first to introduce them to the musical world at large. And it was due to Joachim's matchless presentation and interpretation of them that these compositions became a fundamental pillar of violin literature. We find one or another of the Bach Sonatas or movements from them represented on the programmes of most of the contemporary virtuosos.

Before taking up the "Six Sonatas" individually, we must consider a single movement of one among them, whose over-

---

* Johann Sebastian Bach's greatest contributions to the literature of the violin, the "Solo Sonatas for Violin" and the "Six Sonatas for Violin and Piano," were not generally known to his contemporaries. Very few of Bach's works were even published during his lifetime, most of them still being in Mss. more than a century after his death, while many have been lost. His works were practically ignored for more than half a century after he died. The Italian composers dominated the field of violin composition toward the middle of the eighteenth century, and that Bach was acquainted with their works is shown by his transcribing sixteen Vivaldi violin concertos for the pianoforte and four for the organ. These somewhat bare originals he transformed by the power of his genius into true masterpieces. As Wasielewski says: "If we compare the Vivaldi Concerto in the private library of the King of Saxony with Bach's (piano) transcription, we can see what has happened to the Italian composer's dry skeleton. It seems as though some magic power had turned a meagre grassplot into an attractive flower-bed!" Bach's immortal original "Sonatas," however, are altogether his own; yet as we have said, their influence did not make itself felt until long after their creator had passed away.

powering and elementary grandeur, and unity of conception
makes it an absolute individual work, though comprised with
other movements in the frame-work of a sonata or partita.

The "Ciaconna" or, if one prefer the French form of the
word, the "Chaconne" from Bach's Fourth Sonata in D
minor, together with its thirty-three variations—because of its
absolute musical value—is one of the most frequently played
among the great master's works. Before discussing the
"Ciaconna" and its interpretation in detail, we should mention
that the Bach Sonatas, unlike those of Corelli and Tartini,
were not born directly "out of the violin" itself. They were
not, in first instance, a direct "violin" product, but a product
of pure inspiration, of the highest idealistic invention, and since
they occasionally wellnigh ignore the limitations of what is
violinistically possible, they offer the player some of the greatest
problems to be found in the whole range of violin technique.
It has been said and truly that these Sonatas, "notably in the
movements in polyphonic style, represent the victory of the
spirit over material limitations," and this applies especially to
the "Ciaconna."

I cannot forbear quoting in part the admirable description
Spitta, in his "Johann Sebastian Bach," a work which the
violinist is not ordinarily apt to consult has given of the "Ciaconna," since it is one which will help the student realize its
emotional content in his playing: "The flooding wealth of
figuration pouring forth from a few, hardly noticeable sources,
betrays the most exact knowledge of violin technique, as well
as the most absolute control of an imagination more gigantic,
perhaps, than any an artist has possessed. We must remember
that it is all written for a single violin! And yet what does
this little instrument not allow one to experience! We move
from the serious grandeur of the beginning through the gnaw-
ing restlessness of the Second Theme to the thirty-seconds
driving demoniacally up and down, and veiling the outline of
the Third Theme in a sinister shroud. Again, from those
quivering arpeggios which, moving in a hardly noticeable manner hang like a cloudy veil above a gloomy mountain ravine,
yet which a wind blowing with greater power now drives
together and gathering them in a thick ball whips them roaring

into the tree-crests, so that the latter bend groaning in one and another direction as their torn leaves are whirled about, we progress to the solemn beauty of the movement in D major, in which the radiance of the evening sun falls into the valley. This golden radiance flows through the air, the waves of the stream run gold and mirror the picture in the sky's dome, rising majestically into space immeasurable. The master's spirit inspires the instrument to express the inconceivable; at the end of the D major movement the music wells like organ-tone, at times one hears a whole chorus of violins."

The "Ciaconna" is unquestionably one of the most difficult violin compositions to *perform in public!* We have to take into consideration that aside from the technical factor, a really profound musical understanding is necessary in order to allow each Variation to unfold its own individual character, and to preserve the deeply dramatic quality of the entire work and thus make it comprehensible to the listener. Besides, there are various external difficuties which have to be taken into account:

1. There is the matter of memory. Ordinarily, when playing with piano* or orchestra accompaniment, the solo artist has a musical support which helps him over many little memnotic weaknesses; in the case of the "Ciaconna" the very slightest lapse of memory would at once stand out and distract from the effect of the whole performance.

2. Another vital problem is that of making the strings stay in tune in a crowded hall. To return once more to the matter of the accompaniment: ordinarily we would say that a solo player can tune his strings during the intermissions played by piano or orchestra, but in the case of the "Ciaconna" it is utterly impossible to tune the violin during the performance. There remains only a choice of playing on strings which are out of tune with as much purity of intonation as the exertion of the greatest effort will allow, or of breaking off at the end of a Variation in order to tune the strings, thus completing the performance under difficulties.

---

* Though two great composers, Schumann and Mendelssohn, have exhausted their ingenuity in inventing adequate piano accompaniments for the "Ciaconna," every violinist instinctively feels that it is a work essentially complete in itself, a *solo* work for the violin which needs no support.

I always advise my pupils *never* to play the "Ciaconna" at the *beginning* of a recital or concert, but to introduce it in the *middle* of the programme, so that it will be possible for the violin—or rather the strings—to adapt themselves to the temperature of the hall in question.

Neither at the beginning of the work nor in the course of the Variations do we find a tempo indicated. I would suggest the tempo *Grave* for the Theme itself. With regard to the Variations, I already have stated that each Variation should be given its individual character in performance, the more so since the movements of all the Bach Sonatas are characteristic pieces, musically speaking. I might add that this result must be secured by hardly noticeable modifications in tempo and by means of the most varied tone-colorings. The chords at the beginning of the "Ciaconna" must not be played as we often hear them played, in a *divided* manner. For instance:

but they must be played *firmly*, with a full tone, thus:

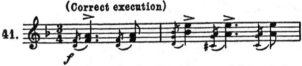

yet without any scratchy, rosiny tonal by-product!

With regard to the tempo and the tone-color, in general, they remain unchanged until the letter **B*** is reached, at which point the Second Variation begins, a Variation that should be played with gentle sentiment, *expressivo*, and a shade more quietly as regards tempo.

From letters **D** and **E** on the interpretation should assume a decidedly more energetic character, up to the letter **F**, at which point a somewhat quieter tempo once more should be observed. At letter **G** a most energetic *forte*, in strict time,

---

* The letters here cited are those given in my complete edition of Bach's "Six Sonatas for Solo Violin," published by Carl Fischer, Inc., New York.

should be observed up to the fourth measure before letter **I**.
There a sudden *piano* with a swell or *crescendo* in the scales is
indicated, which lasts until the following passage:

is reached, where the violinist again plays quietly and softly
up to the letter **K**. At letter **K** a decided *pp* is noted, and
the entire Variation assumes a certain dreaminess of mood
until, gradually, a powerful *crescendo* leads over to Variation
L, which should be played in the tempo indicated for the
beginning.

The Variations which follow progress in ascending and
descending cadences at practically the same tempo, with a
ritenuto and a powerful *crescendo* up to one measure before
letter **P**, where strict time is once more to be observed, while
at the sixth measure of this Variation the tempo broadens out
in organ-style:

as at the beginning.

At letter **Q**:

a similar organ effect occurs (here the solo violinist should
strive to imitate the organ *pianissimo*, maintained very quietly
until the letter **R** is reached, where a somewhat livelier tempo
may be developed. This slightly more movemented tempo
lasts until we come to the second measure before the letter **W**.
There a *crescendo* of decided power leads to a *fortissimo:*

which suddenly drops into *mezzo-forte* in order to make possible a succeeding *forte* and the *fortissimo*, at letter **Z**.

At **Aa** the phrase closes with a *fortissimo*, and begins again quietly on the second quarter of the measure:

moving on without change until we reach **Bb**, where we have an added *expressivo* which is carried through to **Cc**. The four measures which follow serve as a preparation for **Dd**, where the great organ-point, beginning *piano*, works up uninterruptedly in tonal power to lead to the climaxing point of the whole composition at **Ff**. A final Variation, at *Sempre più forte*, carries us to **Gg**, where the violin—just as though it were an organ—presents the original theme with the *utmost employ of tonal power*, in a *fortissimo;* the composition ending in a serious and dignified style with a short piano ══════ *fortissimo.*

A consideration of the Bach Sonatas for Solo Violin would begin naturally with the Sonata in G minor No. 1. In my edition* the time signature for the *Adagio* is given as 16/16, instead of the more usual Common Time (4/4), in order to facilitate playing the rhythmic introduction. If all the eighth-notes, sixteenth-notes, thirty-second notes and sixty-fourth notes which occur be divided into *sixteen parts*, then counting at so slow a tempo is far more secure than when counting by *eighths.* And—what is of major importance as regards interpretation—the *melodic* portion of this Prelude stands out more clearly when this division into sixteenths is carried out, playing very slowly. The movement is extremely singable, and it should be played in a singing manner. The thirty-second and sixty-fourth notes are short passages which should be handled as part of the melody-line of the composition. At **C** the music takes on a dramatic development and this mood dominates up to the close.

* "Six Solo Sonatas for the Violin" by Johann Sebastian Bach. Revised and Edited by Leopold Auer. Carl Fischer, Inc., New York.

The Fuge should be taken at a moderate tempo and the player should see to it, in particular, that the theme:

always is clearly enunciated, whether presented *piano* or *forte*, and whether it appear in the *upper* voice, the middle voice or in the *bass*. At **D**, for example, the theme lies in the upper voice, and at **E** in the bass. It should be played with the maximum amount of breadth at **L**, where the theme appears in the bass while the three remaining strings play chords. The Fuge makes a deep impression when played in the manner indicated, and when the dynamic marks prescribed are followed with the greatest exactness.

The "Siciliana" in B flat major, which follows is a beautiful singing number, beautifully worked out and very colorful if the two voices which continually return:

(the upper voice frequently is embellished with thirds and sixths) are differentiated, and the accompanying bass (in most cases moving on the G string) is clearly and distinctly marked.

The concluding *Presto* movement is a brilliant musical composition and an excellent study for *détaché* and *spiccato* bowing. Only an exact observance of the *nuances* of shading indicated when playing it will permit it to produce the desired impression upon the auditor.

The Second Sonata in B minor is in the form of a suite,* and comprises six movements of varying length, of which two in dance rhythm, the "Sarabande and Double" and, especially, the "Tempo di Bourrée and Double" deserve particular attention. Both the "Sarabande" and the "Bourrée" are old French dances, of which the first demands a somewhat leisurely

---

* It is in fact a suite, and yet the word "sonata" is not incorrectly used to describe all six of the works. Bach himself called Nos. 1, 3, and 5 "Sonatas," and gave the name "Partitas" to the Sonatas 2, 4 and 6. The word "Partita" is a synonom for "suite," but—the Italians called a suite a *sonata da camera* or "chamber sonata," to distinguish it from the regular *sonata da chiesa*, "church sonata." Hence the "Partitas" are quite correctly "chamber sonatas," and the custom of centuries has approved the title "Sonata" for all six of these works for solo violin.

tempo, an approximate Andante, while the "Bourrée" had best be played *Moderato assai*. In both cases the "Double" should be played somewhat more rapidly,** since from a musical point of view the graceful character of the variations demands a somewhat livelier tempo. The expression marks as well as the dynamic signs should be emphasized in the most conscientious manner in order that the player by so doing, may feel certain that he will be able to approach as closely as possible the expression of the composer's meaning.

The Third Sonata, in A minor, like the First Sonata, consists of four movements independent one from the other, and resembles the G minor sonata not alone in its form, but also in the grouping of its movements. The first movement, *Grave-Lento*, also enters in 16/16 time; it also has its dramatic moments, and in no wise yields to the G minor Sonata as regards melodic beauty. The same might be said of the Fuge, *Moderato assai*—Johann Mattheson (1681-1764) preferred it to the Fuge of the G minor Sonata—which, fortunately, probably owing to the material used, is more extended, something which only adds to the value of the work as a whole. The third movement, *Andante sostenuto cantabile*, is one of Bach's loveliest slow movements and especially rich in melodic invention; together with the *Allegro* which follows it, this is a number often listed on the modern recital programme. I should like to remind the young student that the composer has added to the *Andante sostenuto* the word *cantabile*, i. e., "in a singing manner." The wonderful melody in the upper voice is now and again alternately combined with an accompanying melody on the G and on the D string; and the technical difficulty for the right arm lies in the fact that the *two* melodies must be treated as a *unit;* while at the same time the lead melody must be made to stand out, and the accompanying melody must be more subdued, must be kept discretely in the background.

** The fact that the "Double"—the transformation or variation of a theme in these earlier forms—retained the melody, key and rhythm of its theme, does not mean to say that the *tempo* could not be modified. This earlier type of variation, in the case of variations by Mozart and Beethoven, shows the strongest contrasts of harmony, key and rhythm.

The fourth movement, the *Allegro*, forms a worthy contrast to the preceding *Andante sostenuto*. Expression marks, such as *espressivo*, *ritenuto*, etc., and dynamic signs ◁◁◁◁◁ *f* ▷▷▷▷▷ *crescendo*, *diminuendo*, *piano*, *pianissimo*, must be exactly observed.

The Fourth Sonata in D minor, from the standpoint of form is, of course, a 'suite." It consists of movements in dance-rhythms, "Allemande," "Corrente," "Sarabande" and "Giga" and the great "Ciaconna'" with the 33 variations which already have been considered. The grandeur of the "Ciaconna," and the musical importance of the "Sarabande" and "Giga" cast the first two movements, the "Allemande" and the "Corrente" into the shade. The latter are seldom if ever played in public.

The "Sarabande," in view of its singing character, should retain a *Molto moderato* movement, while the "Giga"—an Italianized form of the old English "Jig," in spite of the fact that it is written in D minor—ought to be played in a decidedly lively tempo, such as an *Allegro assai*.

The Fifth Sonata in C major is perhaps the most important of the six in conception and content, and because of the manner in which the first two movements have been laid out. Its "Fuga," in spite of its length, is probably the most important of the three fugues, in G minor, A minor and C major respectively. To play it properly the player must be equipped with an independently perfected technique of *both* hands, and especial attention must be paid the *quality* of the tone emitted. The leading of the themes, too, demands profound musical understanding, and an exact observance of dynamic signs. There are moments in the "working-up" of the Fugue when the slightest pressure in the right hand *beyond* the absolutely natural degree of pressure called for results in a disagreeable tonal buzzing, which may escape the player's notice but makes a most unfortunate impression on the auditor.

In this connection I should like most emphatically to call the young student's attention to the danger which lurks in the natural wish to produce a big, powerful tone. A big tone has its cause of being, its basis, first: in the physical construction of the hands and their muscular equipment and secondly: in the *manner* in which they are employed, the *school* they represent.   Yet no one theory has adequately solved this important problem, in spite of hundreds of pages of printed matter devoted to it in the form of numerous special studies which attempt to offer solutions.   In addition to the necessary *physical* prerequisites, only natural born *talent* and proper *demonstration* on the teacher's part of *how* the essentials already mentioned should be applied *practically* secure the desired result.   In the third and fourth movements, the *Largo expressive* in F major, which moves in one uninterrupted course, and the *Allegro*, suffer from the crushing importance of the two principal movements .

The Sixth Sonata, in E major, like the two other "Partita" sonatas, assumes the form of a suite made up of dance-forms, with the exception of the "Preludio."   As is well-known this Prelude forms the instrumental introduction to a cantata for chorus, soli and orchestra; while violinistically speaking it remains one of the loveliest, most difficult and technically most useful compositions in this entire sonata group.   It is especially valuable, in view of the incomparable practice it affords for the use of the right wrist in connection with the forearm.   How lofty the level of violin-playing must have been in general, and what a notable violinist—quite aside from his mastery as an organist—Johann Sebastian Bach must have been in order to invent and to play works such as this Prelude and the Fugues in G minor, A minor and C major!

The "Loure" which follows the "Preludio" supplies an equally fine introduction for the charming, merry "Gavotte" in E major, which should be played in a *Tempo moderato*, the historically approved tempo for this old French dance as well as for the "Menuetto."   In the case of this last movement a very moderate tempo also is in place, to make possible the graceful movements of the dancers.   As a model for the style and tempo in which this "Menuetto" should be played we have an example in Mozart's "Don Giovanni" Menuet, which has been handed down by the French balletmasters of the eighteenth century in Europe as a spiritual legacy.   The two "Menuetti"—which seem to take the place of a "Sarabande" —are followed by a "Bourrée" and a jolly "Giga," whose character already has been described. The entire "Partita" or "Sonata" in E major, when played in an artistic manner, is one of the most characteristic and grateful works which may be included in a recital programme.

Among Bach's other original compositions for violin the two Concertos, respectively in E major and A minor call for mention. In my "Violin Playing As I Teach It" I already have expressed my individual opinion with regard to these two compositions. I have said that with the exception of the two slow middle movements which demonstrate Johann Sebastian Bach's genius, especially the slow movement of the E major Concerto, these works cannot claim to rank with the Master's other violin compositions,* either musically, or as regards virtuoso interest or pedagogic value.

Unquestionably Bach's most important work in this *genre* is his Concerto in D minor for two violins: it is rich in invention from its beginning to its last note, and the middle movement stands out by reason of its wonderful duo between the two violins. It exists in various excellent editions published by German and by American publishers. I myself have heard the Concerto played in an unforgettable manner by Eugène Ysaye and Mischa Elman in New York. As they played it, it did not represent a battle for supremacy between two great solo artists. Each player was absorbed by the work itself, each surrendered himself to the work as a whole, without for a moment forgetting the requirements of an ideal, perfected reproduction, musically and technically.

Not only is this Concerto one of the most touching and moving numbers in all violin literature, but it also contains one of the loveliest of those melodies which Bach's genius created as a heritage of beauty for the generations to come. The

---

* There is a Concerto in G minor, by Bach, for Violin with accompaniment of string orchestra and organ edited by Tivadar Nachez, which is of real musical interest. Mr. Nachez quite properly has called his work a "reconstruction to its original violin form." Bach's original violin concerto was transcribed by him for the clavier, a half-tone lower, into F minor; in the Nachez version it is once more put into G minor and the arrangement has been made with all reverence for the spirit of the work, Bach's own orchestration being retained, and an organ part taking the place of the original harpsichord, which does not "sound" on the modern concert platform. The Concerto shows the influence of Vivaldi. The initial *Allegro molto moderato*, in two-four time, and the concluding *Presto* in three-eight time, both in G minor are decidedly effective; but to my thinking the most beautiful of the three movements is the Largo in B flat major, in four-quarter time, which ending in G major is a tenderly expressive uninterrupted violin *cantilena* embellished with the richest ornamentation, and a wonderful study for sustained playing.

Third Movement, *Allegro*, is a masterpiece of counterpoint and, quite aside from its lyric moments this *Finale* contains delightfully humorous sections which lend it an extraordinary wealth and splendor of color.

The performance of the Bach Double Concerto in D minor calls for two violinists thoroughly imbued with the musical content and importance of the work, and whose technical apparatus allows them to do justice to the composer's intentions. I say this with special reference to the younger generation, which will do well to study this work seriously, and allow itself to be influenced in its own playing by listening to the interpretation given it by outstanding masters of the violin.

The Double Concerto in D minor, however, must never be considered a *solo* composition for *two* solo violinists instead of for *one*. It must be played in accordance with the ideals of chamber music, in which no distinction is made between the first and the second violin as such, the terms "first" and "second" in this case being purely external designations, since it is not possible, of course, to write for *two first* or *two second* violins. It is the value of the musical ideas in *themselves*, and not in connection with one or another of the solo voices which is the determining factor in presentation. The players must comply with this law of art and, whenever the given moment may occur, subordinate themselves to the guidance of the leading voice.

There are Bach transcriptions for violin with piano accompaniment, but they are not numerous. Perhaps the oldest and most famous is the "Aria" from the D major suite for string orchestra, transcribed by August Wilhelmj. It is one of the happiest and most generally played of all transcriptions. Its interpretation, first of all, demands control of a fine singing tone on the violinist's part; this, together with a good Italian master-instrument (or an adequate copy) should enable him to produce the desired effect.

A "Siciliano"* transcribed from a sonata originally for cembalo and flute is an intimately held composition of real charm which often is listed on the concert programmes of Jascha Heifetz.

---

* "Siciliano," from Johann Sebastian Bach's Sonata for Cembalo and Flute. Transcribed and edited by Leopold Auer. J. H. Zimmerman, Leipsic.

Excellent examples of good Bach transcriptions, in which the piano accompaniments are worked out in harmony with the spirit of the solo parts are the "Two Bourrées"† arranged by Michael Press; and the "Siciliano"—a lovely bit of melody— the sonorous "Arioso" and the "Badinerie" by the master, transcribed by Sam Franko.†† As well as the Adagio from the Organ Toccata in C major arranged by Alexander Siloti.†††

CHAPTER III.

MOZART AND HANDEL.

One must love Mozart and reproduce his music with absolute and intimate conviction if it is to make the desired impression upon the auditor. Mozart wrote his five violin concertos in 1775, under the influence of the French "galant" style of composition, but he gave them the unmistakable impress of his own genius. Of Mozart's concertos the Concerto in D major (No. 4), the Concerto in A major (No. 5), and the Concerto in E flat major are probably the most finished and beautiful, though the Concerto in G contains a wonderful *Adagio*.

In Mozart's Concerto in D major* there are no striking contrasts, no violent *stretti* leading to great climaxes. Its music is uniformly bathed in a mild, golden radiance of sunshine with only a rare cloudlet now and again showing upon the horizon. Its mood is one of joy and merriment, the mood of youth itself, for Mozart was only nineteen years old when he wrote it. Happiness is the keynote of the entire composition and it should be played joyously and happily.

---

† Johann Sebastian Bach, Two Bourrée's. Transcribed for Violin and Piano by Michael Press. Schlesinger, Berlin.

---

†† Johann Sebastian Bach, Siciliano, Arioso, Badinerie. Transcribed for Violin and Piano by Sam Franko. G. Schirmer, Inc.

---

††† Johann Sebastian Bach, Adagio from Organ Toccata in C Major. Transcribed by Alexander Siloti, Carl Fischer, Inc.

---

* Wolfgang Amadeus Mozart. Concerto in D major (No. 4) for violin and piano. Revised and edited by Leopold Auer. Carl Fischer, Inc., New York.

In the first movement, *Allegro*, after an exposition of the themes by the orchestra, the solo violin begins with the Principal Theme:

a fresh, merry motive, full of the joy of life. In the middle of the eighth measure after the letter **B** we find a *dolce, ma espressivo*:

followed by an ascending scale which leads to the energetic close of this short phrase which began so delicately. At letter C another short "song section" sets in, *tranquillo, dolce*:

which after eight measures already yields to the energetic A major phrase:

The two motives last mentioned are absolutely different one from the other, each in its own way, and the player should do his best to express this difference, in part by variety in shading, in part by unnoticeable modifications of tempo. The first theme should be played delicately and quietly as indicated; the second (A major theme) with decisive expression as regards tone and, naturally, in a somewhat more animated tempo.

At the seventh measure after letter **D** there appears for the first time what I am inclined to call a "teasing" passage, two measures long:

In order to secure the "teasing" effect it might be well to play this passage holding back a trifle, and giving each of the quarter-notes a slight accentuation. After letter **E** we have the first three measures in minor:

Apparently the mood here is a trifle sad, but in the very next measure:

it moves merrily into A major. The entrance of the solo violin after letter **F**, at the third measure becomes slightly agitated:

as well as somewhat more animated in tempo; and in order to retain this *agitato* quality I would advise that the *agitato* character be further retained from letter **G** to **H**. From this letter on the various themes for the most part repeat in the tonic until the Cadenza is reached.

The Cadenza begins in a *very moderate* tempo, and keeps its *cantabile*, its "singing" character until we come to the *Allegro* in F major which very energetically, yet with a beautiful quality of tone, should once more present the initial theme of the first movement. The *Allegro vivace* which follows should be played very lightly, with a loose wrist up to the *forte* before the *Moderato*. Then, in continuation, it should be presented with decided breadth to the conclusion of the Cadenza.

The second movement, *Andante cantabile,* like most of Mozart's slow movements, is a fount of the loveliest, most heart-stirring melodies. Only if the player is permeated with its beauty will he be able to give it adequate expression. Although the movement is captioned *Andante* I would advise that it be played somewhat more in the tempo of an *Adagio,* dividing the three-quarters into eighth-rhythms and presenting the movement in a very sustained style. One of its most outstanding moments commences one measure before letter **D**:

and lasts until letter **F**. The Cadenza should be played very broadly and singingly, with the exception of the passage marked *leggiero* and *accelerando:*

The next to last measure of the *Andante* demands a *ritenuto* with a hold or *fermata:*

which, unfortunately, is not indicated.

The last movement of this Concerto, a "Rondeau," *Andante grazioso,* is one that may be said to determine its own expression, musically speaking. It is delicate, intimate, graceful. The eighth notes:

at the beginning should not be given their full value; they should rather be played as follows:

in order to preserve the joyous character of the theme.

The *Allegro, ma non troppo*, letter **A**, must be played very lightly and happily; yet, in spite of the *spiccato* bowing the stroke should come from the wrist, the bow being held with a somewhat firmer grasp so that the player may be better able to control it. Eight measures after letter **C** the eighth note at the beginning of each measure:

should be played as shortly as possible in order to preserve the merry character of the phrase. Letter **D** is a repetition of the *Allegro*. The passage in sixteenths at letter **E** is provided with very exact indications; all that is required is for the player to observe them exactly as they are given; and the same applies to the *Andante grazioso* at letter **F**. From letter **H** on:

the tempo grows somewhat more animated, and a loose *spiccato* bowing should be used. As the case may demand, a slight modification of *tempi* in keeping with the character of the music is permissible until the *Andante* following—six measures before letter **K**—has been reached. The close of the final *Allegro, ma non troppo* creates an impression of a spontaneity full of charm owing to the long sustained *ritenuto* which is continued to the very last note of the composition.

The Concerto in A major* commences with an orchestral introduction which contains no allusion to the *Adagio* with which the solo violin begins. It seems as though the composer

---

* Wolfgang Amadeus Mozart. Concerto in A major, No. 5, for violin and piano. Revised and edited by Leopold Auer. Carl Fischer, Inc., New York.

purposely meant to interrupt the merry orchestral introduction
and the joyous, happy entrance of the solo violin *after* the
short *Adagio*, with a serious moment. It is in this sense that
the *Adagio* should be conceived and played; very quietly and
sustained, with a wave-like movement of the thirty-second notes
in the orchestra. The trill at the end:

should be decidedly long sustained.

The *Allegro aperto* (An *Allegro* clearly and broadly
phrased) is very decided in character, and its rhythmic accents
must be stressed since they bring out the life and vitality inherent in the theme. At the ninth measure after the beginning
of the *Allegro* succeeding the *forte*, we find a sudden *piano*,
with the swelling in the volume of tone indicated in the first
measure of the following example:

and another in the second measure which is several times
repeated.

At letter **B** the first eighth-note must be played shortly, as
well as that in measure three:

The melody which follows should be presented with great
intimacy and without change of tempo. At letter **C** play in
a very light and playful manner, and keep this mood until
letter **D** is reached, where a most expressive melody:

once more appears. At the seventh measure after letter **E** a
new theme is introduced:

68.

f espressivo

with a sorrowful undertone. It is marked *espressivo* and should
be taken in a somewhat quieter tempo. Two measures after
letter **F** the Principal Theme once more reappears as at the
beginning of the *Allegro aperto*. Every violinist is entitled to
play the Cadenza which follows according to his own conception: the tempos change according to the nature and
character of the motives drawn from the first movement of the
concerto, upon which the Cadenza is built.

The second movement, *Adagio*, contains a veritable treasure
of the loveliest melodies, and those who would sound its hidden deeps of beauty, and prepare to do so with true devotion
and self-sacrifice, will enjoy revelations of inestimable musical
value. This entire Concerto in A is not played often enough
in public, no doubt because, though simple in conception and
rich in invention, it demands the manifold colors of the
orchestral accompaniment in order to win proper appreciation.
The *Adagio* should be played in a very sustained manner from
the very start, and the eighth-notes in the 2/4 measure indicated
should be taken quite slowly, since otherwise the thirty-second
notes, which form a very essential part of the melody, will
sound as though they were being hurried, and thus will detract
from the effect. Six measures before the letter **C**:

69.

f

play with great *energy*, and the measure immediately following very *softly*. The repetition of the measure just mentioned
should be carried out in exactly the same way. With this
exception play *forte* until letter **C** has been reached. Four
measures after letter **D** we have a most important moment with

regard to expression: Here the *Agitato*, restless, full of excitation, and also somewhat more movemented in tempo:

continues up to the *Tempo primo*, which again is taken very quietly. Two measures after letter **E** the initial theme of the *Adagio* once more sets in. In the Cadenza after the two measures of trills:

there occurs what I am tempted to call a *scherzoso* passage:

It is one of the motives of the *Adagio* and should be played in that sense, a very light *spiccato* bowing being used for the above measure and the three which follow it.

The third movement of the Concerto is marked *Tempo di Minuetto*, which actually is equivalent to *Tempo moderato*. The motive should be presented *dolce*, with a soft quality of tone, and should be played simply and with *exact* observance of the dynamic signs. The five measures coming a little after letter **C** which follow:

are characterized by a distinct change of mood. The first four measures of the group are to be played with decided harshness, and the measures which follow *piano*, *dolce*, very delicately and teasingly. The Menuet character of the piece is maintained until the *Allegro vivace* in A minor, in 2/4 time, is reached.   It is a genuine *Vivace*, not only with regard to tempo but also as regards expression; the following passage:

should be specially accented.* yet not to such a degree that quality of tone suffers.

In view of the fact that the Menuetto is repeated at various times by the orchestra and the solo violin, I suggest the following "cuts," especially in public performance:

From letter **H** on cut sixteen measures up to the entrance of the solo violin on the third quarter:

Later, at the last quarter before letter **I**, cut eight measures, to the third quarter of the *forte* entrance in the orchestra:

I do not believe that the composition suffers when these "cuts" are made; it is merely a matter of eliding repetitions which unnecessarily extend it.

In the Mozart Concerto in E flat major,† the beginning of the work in the orchestra as well as the two characteristic concluding measures of the introduction (letter **A**) prove that the composer as regards the tempo of the first movement preferred a *Moderato* to an *Allegro*.   With the entrance of the solo violin with the delicate phrase which forms the reply to the two very energetic initial measures of the Principal Theme this preference is most clearly marked.

---

* With regard to the *spiccato* and other types of bowing the student is referred to my "Violin Playing As I Teach It."   Frederick A. Stokes Co., New York.

---

† Wolfgang Amadeus Mozart. Concerto in E flat major for Violin and Piano. Revised and edited by Leopold Auer.   G. Schirmer, New York.

At letter **C** we have the Second Theme:

equally delicate and songful, which passes over into the orchestra, where it serves as the basis for a graceful passage by the solo violin, one which grows more energetic at letter **D**, and builds up to a *forte*. At letter **E** a new theme in C minor, a theme decidedly masculine in character appears, and not till eight measures later do we have a gentler moment which lasts for a few measures:

but which soon, by means of a *crescendo*, leads over into a *forte* interlude by the orchestra. At letter **I** the first (Principal) Theme once more appears, with a small sequential change; in this connection I must not forget to warn the student that the three high notes:

before the close should not be forced.

In the second movement, *Un Poco Adagio*, in spite of the "*Poco Adagio*" and the 3/4 time indicated, I would advise dividing the quarters into eighths, to produce the sixteenth- and thirty-second notes which form an essential part of the melody more quietly and singingly. When beginning the two measures starting on the note F:

the playing of the two notes with one bow-stroke offers no difficulties in slow tempo if the bow attacks the string lightly,

at the nut, and is managed very carefully so that the player
has enough bow at his disposal to carry out the *crescendo* in
the middle. Eight measures before letter **B**, we come to one
of the noblest musical moments in the work, the passage in
B flat minor:

It cannot be played with too much warmth and feeling. The
close of the movement, following the short Cadenza reverts to
the lyric mood as in the beginning.

The third movement "Rondeau" *(Allegretto)* should be
played according to the indications given, lightly and in the
middle of the bow. This last movement calls for a well-
developed technique in both hands. At letter **A** a broad
détaché without change of tempo should be used; at letter **B**
play somewhat more quietly. Forearm and wrist must com-
bine in elastic movement to do justice to the melody:

which should be produced with a soft, beautiful quality of
tone. At letter **D** the *diminuendo* which leads over to the
Principal Theme is important.

At letter **E**:

play with much warmth of tone and take the sixteenth-note
passage which follows very flowingly. At letter **K** the sixteenths should be played strictly in time and with a big tone
up to four measures before letter **L**, where the *diminuendo*
(as at letter **C**) leads to the Principal Theme. The four concluding measures should be played very lightly and gracefully.

George Friederich Handel's (1685-1759) "Six Sonatas for Violin and Piano"* represent a contribution to violin literature which, though their composer's main achievement lay in other fields, is still an integral part of the violin concert repertoire and one cherished by its greatest exponents at the present day.

Among these "Six Sonatas" I have chosen for consideration the three which are best-known and which most frequently appear on the recital programme. No. 1, in A major; No. 4, in D major; and No. 6, in E major. The Handel sonatas are planned on the same model. They consist of four movements varying in length; two slow movements (first and third) and two rapid, *Allegro* movements (second and fourth). In these Handel compositions, as in all the compositions of his day until the advent of Beethoven, who blazed new trails in musical composition, the *Andante* is equivalent to the contemporary *Adagio*, and its quarter-notes always should be divided into eighths, in order that the movement may preserve its proper character.

This applies in particular to the first movement of the Sonata in A major (No. 1). The second movement (*Allegro*), with its energetic fugal themes, if it is to be properly interpreted, must be played strictly in time, and with exact observance of all accents and dynamic signs wherever indicated. Beginning at letter **F**, the tempo broadens out until the end of the movement is reached. The third movement, *Adagio*—in spite of the repetition prescribed—is too short, and is practically no more than an introduction for the last movement, *Allegro*, with respect to its tempo and rhythm a species of *Gigue*. The student should be careful to stress the *sudden changes* from *forte* to *piano*, changes which are entirely unprepared; that is, unprovided with a *diminuendo* from the *forte* to the *piano* and, *vice versa*, a *crescendo* from the *piano* to the *forte*.

The first movement of the Sonata in D major (No. 4) has been planned on broader lines than those of the corresponding movement of its companion in A major. It is marked *Adagio*,

---

* G. F. Handel. "Six Sonatas for Violin and Piano." Revised and edited by Leopold Auer. Carl Fischer, Inc., New York.

and its eighth-notes should be played more slowly than those
in the *Andante* of the sonata just considered. The *Allegro*
which succeeds this initial *Adagio* is equally important in form
and content. The third movement, *Larghetto*, is reminiscent
of some of the loveliest arias of Handel's operas and oratorios.
It stands to reason that the more broadly the eighth-notes are
played, the more intimately and beautifully will this aria be
produced. At the fifth measure after letter **B** I advise an
almost unnoticeable *accelerando:*

'84.

up to the *forte,* and thenceforward a reversion to the preceding broadly expressive tempo until the end of the movement.
The concluding *Allegro*, rhythmically as well as melodically,
resembles a menuet of the more animated type, and should
be played with spirited expression.

The Sonata in E major (No. 6) is externally, with regard
to its form, identical with the two sonatas already considered.
It differs from them, however, in its inner building-up; for in
it we find neither contrapuntal nor fugal development. This,
however, in no wise interferes with the natural flow of the
composer's invention. On the contrary, it seems to me that
the melodic charm of the work is thereby enhanced. The
Adagio, its first movement, if presented with its proper meed
of expression, makes a profound impression on the listener.
The second movement, *Allegro*, bubbles over with life and
vitality, and is one of the most precious sonata-movements of
its kind. The interpreter must see to it that the pulsing vitality
of this movement is duly expressed in his playing. The third
movement, *Largo*, moves *at least* on the same plane of musical
beauty as its predecessor. In order to bring both player and
auditor to a more intimate realization of its loveliness I call
for its repetition in my edition of the work; so that the first
time the movement is played an octave lower, and the repeat
carried out as originally written. The final *Allegro*, with its
prickling, effervescent movement, supplies a worthy conclusion

for these three sonatas. Eight measures after letter **B** occurs a sequence:

which if properly presented decidely heightens the effect. This passage, after the preceding *forte*, should begin with the most supreme delicacy—I might almost say *tenderness* of expression—and after the four measures during which this *piano* is maintained should broaden out in a swell of tone which terminates in the *forte* at letter **C**. The remainder of the movement should be played according to the indications given.

CHAPTER IV.

BEETHOVEN'S "KREUTZER" SONATA AND HIS "ROMANCES."

Before discussing the Beethoven "Kreutzer" Sonata in detail it seems in order to set down a few reflections regarding the interpretation of chamber music* in general. In the case of compositions in sonata form written for several instruments—in this specific instance for violin and piano—there is *no difference* between the instruments in question with regard to their *respective importance* in the interpretation of the work. Both have absolutely equal rights, and the composer decides which of the two instruments is the leading instrument for the time being. The experienced musician who is guided by genuinely musical principles will follow his artistic instincts without loosing sight of the composer's intentions. The young, inexperienced aspirant must try to divine these intentions and, above all, must train himself to regard the *composition* itself and its proper interpretation as his goal. He should not thrust his instrument into the foreground at inopportune moments in order to make himself appear as *persona grata*.

---

* The "Kreutzer" Sonata is the one Beethoven Sonata for violin and piano which is included in the concert repertoire of the violin. The remaining sonatas for violin and piano are essentially chamber music and do not come within the scope of the present volume.

Chamber music is the noblest branch of musical art since it attains the loftiest musical heights while employing the most modest means, when these means have been supplied by a masterhand. Opera and the symphony orchestra have at their command a number of factors which help them capture the musical layman's attention. In opera, especially, there are the arts of decoration, of scenic display and costume, the solo male and female voice, as well as the chorus. Besides there is the libretto, which supplies a literary interest, action wedded to gesture in the case of the singers and, finally, the gorgeous colors of the modern orchestral palette.

If we compare with all this the two modest wooden instruments: the piano—for all that its internal fittings are of metal—and the violin, how much more difficult is the task set them, how much more profound the work calling for interpretation must be, and how outstanding the talent of the two players, in order to charm and capture the hearts of their listeners with only these simple means at their command!

Beethoven originally had intended to dedicate the famous "Kreutzer" Sonata for violin and piano, Op. 47, to the English violinist Bridgewater, but when Rudolph Kreutzer,* the author of the "Etudes" made his acquaintance in Vienna in 1798, the master changed his mind and dedicated the work to him.

The first movement of the "Kreutzer" Sonata, like the two "Romances" by the same composer, commences with a solo for the violin, conceived with great breadth and having a truly Beethovenian touch:

86.

---

* During the past few decades this famous Sonata was largely discussed in all civilized countries, and especially in Russia because of Count Leo Tolstoy's novel, "The Kreutzer Sonata." The founder and director of the Moscow Conservertory of Music, Nicolas Rubinstein, long since dead, one day told me how Count Tolstoy happened to give his well-known book this title. "Count Tolstoy hunted me up one day," Nicolas Rubinstein said to me, "and, among other things asked me to tell him which ensemble work for violin and piano, in my opinion, might be considered the most important. I answered off-hand that I thought Beethoven's Sonata Op. 47, called the "Kreutzer" Sonata because it had been dedicated to the violinist Rudolphe Kreutzer, might deserve to be so called. Not long afterward Tolstoy's novel by this title appeared, and attracted great attention in the literary and in the musical world." I remember Nicolas Rubinstein saying, in a joking way, that he considered himself the godfather of the sensational book.

which lends the whole introduction a certain quality of mystery. Then, after the piano has repeated the four measures in A minor, both instruments join in presenting the theme, which dies away in the long *pianissimo* leading over to the *Presto*.

As I have already remarked elsewhere no composer has supplied so great a number of dynamic signs in his works as Beethoven, a strong proof of how much stress he laid on their exact observance. In this short introduction, only *eighteen* measures long, we find *sixteen* different dynamic indications! With regard to changes in tempo, however, the genial master has been less exact, if we except such absolutely essential indications as *poco ritenuto*, *ritenuto*, *a tempo*, the *General Pause* and, as goes without saying, the tempo indication at the beginning of the various movements of his work.

The *Presto* movement is greatly agitated, with continuous outbursts of passion as at letter **A**:

At letter **B** the chords should be played shortly and sharply at the nut of the bow, and in a very flexible manner, from the wrist, in order to avoid any scratchy secondary flavor. At letter **C** the magnificent singing theme:

begins in a somewhat quieter tempo. After the General Pause at letter **D**, the music reverts to its already mentioned agitated and excited character, and this mood is especially marked twelve measures after letter **E**:

whence it continues in an even more agitated and exalted strain, if possible, until the repetition:

has been reached.

At letter **G** the working-out begins in the piano, while in the violin part we have supporting allusions:

to the preceding Second Theme. The *expressivo, piano*, which would be in place here is missing in my edition; yet when it is played *forte* the clearness of the two voices is diminished. The other dynamic signs are correctly indicated and should be closely observed.

At letter **K**, a tempestuously ascending Cadenza ends on a *pianissimo* hold *(fermata)*, leading back to the Initial Theme, which introduces the same motives which are presented in the first, smaller section of the First Movement; this time, however, in different keys, as is usual in the sonata form. At the letter S the figure in eighths:

is based on the short piano chords which, after a long sustained *forte* and *sforzando* lead, by means of a sudden *forte-piano*, *decrescendo* and *pianissimo*, to a lovely modulation in B flat major and thence, ever ascending, to a tremendous climax:

After the hurricane has died away the *Adagio:*

appears in the violin like a quivering ray of golden sunlight.
When the piano has repeated these four measures in the tonic,
the movement ends with a violent recapitulation of the figure
in eighths already mentioned, on this occasion presented in
alternation by the violin and the piano in a swift, decisive
Tempo primo.

In the Second Movement of the Kreutzer Sonata, the
Andante con variazioni, the piano introduces a lofty, simple
melody, profoundly expressive, its first eight measures repeated
by the violin. Here, too, in these few phrases, we find one
of those touches which Beethoven alone supplies, in measures
4 and 5 of the violin part:

and I cannot recommend too emphatically that the student
observe this sudden *piano* following the *crescendo.* This detail
of shading can be carried out to best advantage if the bow be
slightly raised from the string *after* the G sharp, and then
softly returned to it for the F natural, without allowing the
rhythm to suffer.

The first Variation is a piano variation, with a seemingly
simple accompanying figure in the violin. Yet the violin figure
is simple only in appearance. I have indicated various bowings for the triplet: above the note I have put − − − to indicate
a light *détaché,* and below the note ⌣ • ⌣ • ⌣ i. e., a very light
ascending "flying" *staccato.* The violinist may use either of
the two bowings indicated according to whether the pianist
plays *his* triplets long or short. The violin, since it is the
secondary instrument in this variation, must follow the piano
exactly, and breathe simultaneously with it, using a greater or
lesser degree of power. It is for this reason that the violin
part in this variation is unprovided with any dynamic signs.

50 VIOLIN MASTER WORKS

The Second Variation is a violin variation and is full of grace. From a technical point of view it represents a very difficult task for both hands. I myself have been in the habit of playing it with a different bowing when repeating the two sections; first playing it:

and when making the repetition as follows:

with a light *staccato* produced with an absolutely loose wrist. The second section should be played as indicated.

The Third Variation, in F minor, calls for a larger degree of dramatic expression, especially in measures 4, 5 and 6:

This phrase is repeated at the close of the variation, and in view of its serious character the entire variation may appropriately be played in a *Tempo poco meno mosso*.

The Fourth Variation, which returns to F major, is conceived in a very joyous mood, and has a somewhat Mozartean tinge which it keeps until letter E has been reached. From this point on, with the theme played in the violin on the E string, and the subsequent Cadenzas in the piano part and later in the violin part, the lion's claws once more are unsheathed. At letter F, after the long trill in the violin, both player and auditor experience a sensation of redemption and release after deep suffering. A few measures after letter G the trill occurs in both instruments. It should be remembered that Beethoven does not demand an "after-beat," a gracenote, in the violin trill. When playing in public I always have con-

tinued my trill on the upper E until the pianist has concluded
his trill on G sharp:

99.

(Piano)

Then, once more united, we ended the movement very quietly
as indicated.

The *Finale*, *Presto*, of the "Kreutzer" Sonata is joyous,
merry and quite unrestrained, with tarantella-like themes —
such is the character of a movement which stands alone in the
literature of chamber music. Unfortunately, this fine composition is often "rushed along" when played on the concert
platform. The layman even seems to be impressed by such
gallopades, for all that distinctness in the passage-work and
musical clarity must go by the board. The violin presents the
Principal Theme at the beginning, and it is taken over by the
piano after eight measures, while the violin has the second
part. This exchange of the voices recurs until the letter **B** is
reached, where the playfully teasing Second Theme:

100.

appears in the violin. It should be played at the *point* of the
bow, *piano*, yet sharply marked, as a *martelé* stroke. When
the piano takes over this theme the violin develops a graceful
accompanying figure:

101.

played *spiccato*, and as delicately and lightly as possible.

At letter **D**, after a preceding *ff*, which is sustained for
several measures ,we have a *sudden piano*. In the second section of the *Finale* the principal mood is the same as the first.
At letter **H** we have a place which presents some difficulties

with regard to the ensemble of the two instruments.   These
difficulties are especially noticeable after the eighth measure:

where the piano assumes the lead, and the violin using a light
spiccato, must very carefully subordinate itself to the keyed
instrument.   At letter **M** we have a repetition of the important
shading discussed when it first occurs at letter **E**; on this occasion, however, it appears in the tonic.   Before letter **P** we find
two *sudden Adagios*, interrupted by two equally sudden
Tempi primi.   These changes of tempo are very typical of
Beethoven.   The *Adagio* represents a genuine "catching of
the breath" in the midst of the preceding tempestuous hurricane
whirl, and hence must be played without *preparation*, by which
I mean without a *ritenuto* and, when it precedes the *Tempo
primo, without* a preparatory *accelerando*.   In my opinion it
is only by interpreting the passage in this wise that it is possible to carry out the genial composer's manifest wish and
intention.   At letter **P**, finally, we storm onward without a
break to the three closing chords.

Beethoven's "Romances"* for violin and piano are two in
number, the first, Op. 40, in G major, the second, Op. 50, in
F major.   The "Romance in G" begins with a Principal
Theme for solo violin in double stops, which are anything but
easy to play, instead of with the more customary exposition of
the theme by the orchestra.   The title of the composition suffi-
ciently indicates the composer's intentions: *Romanze* is
synonomous with *Lied*. i. e., "song" in German, hence the
composition is a song from beginning to end.   Beethoven indicates the tempo as *Adagio cantabile*.   After the orchestra
has repeated the two violin solos, it introduces the secondary
theme at letter **A**:

* "Two Romances" (Op. 40, Op. 50) by Ludwig van Beethoven.   Revised and
edited by Leopold Auer.   Carl Fischer, Inc., New York.

The entire composition, until letter **C** is reached, should sound like a tender dialogue, here and there interrupted, and in keeping with this colloquial style should be played with unaffected beauty of tone and expression. With letter **D** the theme in E minor appears:

104.  *etc.*

which, since its energetic character offers a contrast to the preceding lyric theme, should be played "in character." It calls for a tempo somewhat more movemented than that of the Principal Theme. The sixteenth-note figure:

105.

is *not* an ordinary passage, but a variant of the E minor theme. It should be rendered in a very sustained and singable style, as at the beginning. At letter **G** a very beautiful modulation begins on the trill, *piano*, which increasing in intensity is conducted by the orchestra to the following point:

106.

From this climacteric point it carries on more and more quietly until the two closing chords—which Beethoven has provided with the indications *a tempo* and *ff*—have been reached.

The second "Romance," Op. 50, in F major, as regards both its form and its mood, shows a great resemblance to the Romance in G major. Here, too, it is the solo violin which presents the Principal Theme, this time with the accompaniment of the orchestra, however; whereupon the latter repeats the eight measures which resume the motive. Until letter **B** is reached the character of the composition is somewhat contemplative; but subsequent to this letter the melody grows a

little more agitated, supported by the sonorous passages which
end on the two trills:

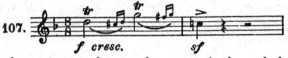

At letter **C** an exchange of contrasts in the melody commences
between the orchestra and the solo violin; the former *forte*,
rough and decisive, and the latter delicate and intimate, growing gradually brighter in tone and leading over to the Principal
Theme by means of a Cadenza two measures long. At letter
E the mood grows a trifle more agitated in the phrase in F
minor:

and retains this character until letter **F** has been reached. Here
begins the preparation:

for the return of the Principal Theme in the solo violin, at
letter **G**. At letter **H**, *piano*, a chromatic scale commences in
sixteenth notes and moves in a steady *crescendo*, interrupted by
a sudden *piano:*

which leads over to the climax:

At this point the violin enters, *dolce*, and growing softer and
softer, delicately brings the composition to a close with a
ritenuto on the F major scale.

Chapter V.
PAGANINI.

All in all, Berlioz's summing up of Paganini's accomplishment as a composer is a very fair one.* He says: "One
could write a volume anent all that Paganini has created in
his works by way of novel effects, ingenious contrivances,
grandiose and elevated forms, and orchestral combinations
unknown before him. His melodies are broad Italian ones,
yet impregnated with a passionate ardor seldom met with in
the best pages of the dramatic compositions of his countrymen.
His harmonies always are clear, simple and extraordinarily
sonorous. His instrumentation is brilliant and, without being
noisy, is full of energy. He often introduces the kettle-drum
in his *tutti* with exceptional skill."

The Paganini Concerto in D major (E flat major), No. 1,
by Niccolo Paganini, is probably superior to his Concerto No.
2, in B minor (these are the only two concertos by Paganini
which have been published), and it exists in two distinct editions. One, edited by Carl Flesch (C. Peters, Leipsic) and
another, abbreviated one, containing only the first movement—
which is the best—revised by August Wilhelmj ** (1883).
Both editions are admirable, each in its own way. Carl Flesch
adheres to the form of the original: three movements, *Allegro
maestoso, Adagio espressivo* and *Rondo*, introducing changes
conforming to contemporary demands in the passages, and sup-
plying an original Cadenza. Wilhelmj has used only the First
Movement, regarding it as the only interesting one, giving it
a modern orchestral setting and harmonization, and providing
it with a Cadenza. The Wilhelmj edition, owing to its more
modern framing, is in most cases used in public performance,
and this edition supplies the text for my considerations.

The work makes no special claim to exceptional profundity
of musical content. Yet it comprises some beautiful themes,
though written in the style and taste of a hundred years ago.
It demands even more than a perfected technique: the player

---
* Hector Berlioz. *Soirées de l'Orchestre.*

** Niccolo Paganini, Concerto No. 1, in D major. Edited and revised by August
Wilhelmj. Carl Fischer, Inc., New York.

must also command a reserve fund of technical accomplishment to offset any possible nervousness on the concert platform.
From a pedagogic point of view the work is an exceptionally
valuable one in specific cases.

In the First Movement *(Allegro Maestoso)*, the Principal
Theme at the beginning has a certain noble, majestic quality,
and in order to do justice to it a broad bow-stroke is called
for on each of the longer notes, together with an energetic
accent which last, unfortunately, is at times ignored. The
succeeding phrase:

should be played with a very singing tone, and delicately. I
would advise playing the passage in thirds:

forte, with a *détaché* the first time, and *piano*, *spiccato* when
repeating it and *not*, as indicated, *mezzo-forte* on *both* occasions!

The Second Theme:

forms a lovely contrast to the preceding rapid scales and the
subsequent passage in thirds. The entrance of the solo violin
after the orchestral intermezzo:

should be regarded as a Recitative, and hence be played with freedom and independence until the following passage on next page:

which should *not* be taken *forte*, as prescribed, but *mezzo-piano, spiccato,* since thus *it will sound much better.* With the scales in sixths and tenths the *détaché* in the *forte* claims its rights, as well as in the following chromatic scale in triplets:

to be played in the manner shown above (as Flesch has indicated in his edition) because of the richer sonority of tones secured. The passage just described returns after having been interrupted by a melodious theme in B major:

The passage in thirds in D major should be played with the exact shadings indicated, i. e., the first time *pianissimo* and the second time *mezzo-forte,* on the D and G strings. The Cadenza, of course, should be rendered free with freedom and spontaneity and *ad libitum;* yet at the same time, in keeping with its serious and most important content, it should begin slowly and the passages should not be unduly hurried, especially the scales in octaves at the close.

In Paganini's Concerto No. 2, in B minor, the concluding movement of the work, the famous "La Clochette" ("The Bell"),* holds its own in the concert repertoire. It owes its name to the fact that the composer—though the movement originally was written in B minor—tuned his violin up a whole tone when playing it in order to emphasize its tone color; so that while the orchestra was playing in B minor, he was playing in A minor. This made it possible for him to secure quite unusual tonal effects on the violin in general, and especially with regard to his harmonics, which were the marvel of those who heard them. Until the following measures of "La Clochette":

119.

which suggest the chiming of a little bell, are reached, neither the Principal Theme not any secondary motive offers anything in any way suggestive of a bell or of the bell-tone.

I am very much inclined to doubt that the *Glockenspiel* (or *jeux de clochettes*, as the French say) was used in the orchestra in Paganini's day and supported him while playing as is customary in our own time in order to emphasize the "bell" effect.**

As a whole "La Clochette" or, if one prefer the Italian title "La Campanella," is in no wise remarkable, either as music or considered from the standpoint of violin technique. It is a composition of medium difficulty which the majority of good violinists can master. In fact, the attention the piece has excited was due in first instance to its title and also, probably, to the extraordinary impression it made on its auditors when the composer himself played it.

---

* Niccolo Paganini. "La Clochette," Op. 7. Revised and edited by Fritz Kreisler.

** Berlioz very rightly says that "bells were introduced in orchestration to secure dramatic rather than musical effects;" and though Mozart employed the *Glockenspiel* in "The Magic Flute," this does not imply that the bells were used in symphony orchestras.

Franz Liszt was so enthusiastic about it that he transcribed it for the piano and it is considered to this day one of his most genial and effective transcriptions, one which so far exceeds its original in musical merit that it has done much to secure for the violin original the popularity it enjoys.

"La Campanella" begins—*Allegretto grazioso*—without any introduction, and its graceful Theme should be presented with a short *piqué* bowing, i. e., *mezzo-staccato* notes played with a single bow. In the second section of the theme, *Meno mosso:*

the player should change to a *saltato stroke*, leading over to the "bell" passage.

After the first *tutti* in the orchestra we encounter a rather attractive motive:

which is later followed by a genuinely idiomatic violin passage in D major: (next movement)

which soon brings us to the Principal Theme and the Coda anticipating the close of the composition.

Musically speaking, Paganini should be judged neither by his Concertos nor by the virtuoso pieces with which he dazzled and captivated the audiences of his own day. He must be judged by his one really notable achievement as a composer, for the collection of "24 Capricci per Violino Solo" (Op. 1) which Paganini has contributed to the violin repertoire is an outstanding musical work. Taken individually the "Caprices" are unequal in value. Fortunately, however, the majority of

them are of genuine worth and importance and to this day no
one who aspires to the higher goals in violin-playing can afford
to neglect studying them.   In many cases their musical content
is so exceptional that masters like Schumann, Liszt and Brahms
have not disdained to transcribe them for the piano.   Kreisler,
Nachez and others have provided various ones among them*
with piano accompaniments and thus have made their performance in recital possible.

The Paganini Caprice No. 24, in A minor,** is among all,
perhaps, the one richest in the variety of the study material
and technical problems which it offers the student, for with the
exception of some more extended passages with up- and down-
bow its twelve variations cover practically every branch of
violin technique.   In revising it I have made but few changes,
but have prescribed tempos which are in accordance with the
character of each one of the twelve variations.   Only in the
last variation did some material alterations seem necessary, and
the Coda had been extended in order to "round out" the composition in a musically satisfactory manner.

As is well known, Paganini possessed slender fingers of
exceptional length,† a physical fact to which his compositions
bear witness, and for this reason students who have small hands
and fingers of normal length find many of his "Caprices" wellnigh unconquerable.   Another instance in point, with regard
to the stretches which occur in his compositions is the famous
set of "Variazioni di bravura" on airs from Rossini's opera
"Moise," for the G-string alone.

---

* Niccolo Paganini. Caprice No. 13; Caprice No. 20; Caprice No. 24.   Revised
and edited by Fritz Kreisler. Caprice No. 14; Caprice No. 22.   Revised and edited
by Eddy Brown. Caprice No. 24.   Revised and edited by Leopold Auer.   There also
exist three notably fine concert arrangements of Paganini Caprices (Trois Morceaux
Caracteristiques d'après Paganini) by the late Max Vogrich.   Recital numbers of
bravura effect and brilliancy, their arranger has provided them with picturesque
titles in keeping with their individual character.   Thus Caprice No. 12 is called
"Voice of the Woods," Caprice No. 10 "Dance of Shadows," and Caprice No. 9
"Chevalier Mousquetaire."

** Niccolo Paganini. Caprice No. 24.   Revised and edited with piano accompaniment, by Leopold Auer.   Carl Fischer, Inc., New York.

---

† Paganini's hand was not an exceptionally large one, but he had greatly developed
the stretching capacity of his long fingers through exercise.   If nature had not
given him long fingers to begin with, however, we doubt whether (as has been claimed)
he could have placed the thumb of his left hand on the middle of the violin neck
and played at will in the first three positions without moving it.

I heard this composition played in public for the first time some sixty years ago, when it was performed by Camille Sivori, who was—according to what was told me—Paganini's only outstanding pupil. Naturally, I was very much interested, and after having made Sivori's acquaintance and seen his small hands and his short fingers, I expressed my surprise that he found it possible to take the tremendous leaps and stretches in the composition already mentioned so perfectly. But Sivori cleared up the mystery. With the greatest amiability—we were in his lodgings—he took from his double violin-case a smaller-sized violin which he told me was an Amati, and which had a single, thin G-String in the very middle of the bridge. This violin not alone enabled him to reduce the difficulties of the bravura composition by a good half, he informed me, but without it he would have been unable to play it at all.

Most of Paganini's other compositions—such as the famous "Le Streghe" ("Witches" Dance"), the "Variations on a Theme by S. Mayr," and the "Variations on *Di tanti palpiti*"—are virtuoso pieces pure and simple, and do not possess the musical values of the "Caprices." The well-known "Perpetuum Mobile," however, is an excellent study for *spiccato* and—when perfectly played—a highly effective number for recital performance.

CHAPTER VI.

LOUIS SPOHR.

Louis Spohr's Eighth Concerto, Op. 47, in A minor (In the Form of a Lyric Scene) takes us back more than a century to the years (1815-1820) when Spohr wrote it and in it created the first and only concerto in the form of a *scena cantante** known at the time.

In Italy in particular this, as well as the composer's other works in the neo-romantic style which were then a novelty, excited justified attention and established Spohr's fame as a virtuoso at a time when Paganini was electrifying all Europe by his incomparable technical gifts and his fantastic personality.

---

* Louis Spohr, Concerto No. 8, Op. 47. Revised and edited by Ferd. Carri. Carl Fischer, Inc., New York.

Spohr's Eighth Concerto in its day had a new element of interest insomuch as it presented technique *as a means to an end*, and not as an end in itself, one calculated to supply its player with a halo of virtuosity. In the case of Spohr, Music herself came first, and all else was secondary. And it is owing to this fact and to its originality of form that the "Lyric Scene" is still included—though only occasionally—in the programmes of some of the most outstanding violin virtuosos of the immediate present. In general, before entering upon the detail of its interpretation, we would ask the student to remember that it calls for great breadth and volume of tone in melody and passage-work, an extraordinary stretching capacity of the fingers, and skill in "a certain varied kind of position shift and flexible smoothness in bowing."

The Concerto begins with a short orchestral Introduction, which leads over into a highly dramatic Recitative ** by the solo violin. This Recitative Spohr composed on the model of the Italian opera and concert arias, very likely as a compliment to the Italians, then dominant in the operatic field, and in view of the fact that at the time Spohr was making his first Italian virtuoso tour.

It is almost impossible to make clear in words just *how* a Recitative of this type should be played. As I have mentioned when considering another Concerto (Max Bruch's Second Concerto in D minor, see p. 110) the player must, first of all, understand exactly what the word "recitative" implies and, in addition, must have a feeling for style in order to be able to find the proper quality of musical and dramatic expression needed.

I would like to establish one general rule which the student should observe: the phrase which contains *no coloratura* (i. e., violin passage-work) for the singer (the player who sings on the strings) should be played in a sustained manner and with changes in tone color. Each note which is provided with a hold, ⌒ , must be *decidedly* long sustained. And just as the long-drawn breath in the case of the singer, so the long drawn-out bow in that of the violinist should be regarded as an

** Every student should have a proper conception of a violin *recitativo*, its meaning and its importance.

advantage.   It might be added that grace notes should be taken very composedly and should not be hurried.

To take the place of the vocal artist's *roulades* Spohr has employed highly interesting violin passages which adapt themselves perfectly to the character of the Recitative.

The Aria proper begins at letter **F**.   Here the student will do well *not* to count three quarters; but to divide his quarter into eighth-notes and *very slow* eighth-notes, incidentally, to prevent the sextolets and thirty-second notes which now and then occur from sounding hurried.

At letter **I** the orchestral prelude should be taken in a somewhat more animated tempo.   Though this change of tempo is *not* indicated in the original score, its correctness is clearly established by the triplet figuration and the contrast in mood between the Aria and its repetition (3/4) after letter **M**.

At letter **K** the solo violin sets in with a very passionate theme:

one impossible to accent too energetically—which, of course, does not imply that the tone should be forced.   This is essential to prevent monotony in expression with regard to the Aria which recurs in a slightly varied form, yet played in the same slow tempo.

At letter **O** we have an *Andante* qualified by the indication "Recitative," hence the performer should present it in *recitativo* style, playing his passages clearly and distinctly and without hurrying; while the double trill in particular should be taken with entire equalization of the two fingers:

With the succeeding *Allegro moderato* we are once more re-
moved to the field of violin technique. It is a very energetic
theme, a genuine Spohr passage comprising various bowings
and short trills. In order to preserve its melodic continuity I
would advise the student to play this passage in the following
manner:

that is to say with the accent not *on* but *after* the trill, as indicated. The same rule holds good for the *piano* repetition,
save that melody and accentuation are to be played *much less
vigorously*.

The scale in tenths beginning in the sixth measure before
letter **R** calls for a light wrist-action across the strings. At
letter **S** we find a cantabile "Intermezzo," which separates
the *Allegro moderato* already mentioned from the one about
to appear in a somewhat varied form. The "Intermezzo"
should be taken in a slightly more quiet tempo:

and given a pronounced lyric character, maintained until letter
U is reached, where the *Allegro moderato* tempo once more
sets in.* The passages after letters **U** and **W**, should be
played as at their initial appearance (letter **G**).

The Cadenza is decidedly noteworthy, both musically and
technically. It begins very slowly and *piano*, and little by
little unfolds with increasing tone and greater breadth of bow.

---

* This tempo indication is also missing in the edition under discussion.

With the *crescendo* the tempo, too, is accelerated until the tenths are reached:

127.

Here a big, sonorous tone is in order; and after the last tenth it is advisable to make a slight pause, ⌢ , and to take the subsequent passage in sixths as quietly as possible. This Cadenza, with the concluding scale in thirds, technically speaking, offers the most difficult task in the entire Concerto. Majesty, dignity, soulful song should characterize the interpretation of the entire work, and the "broad, somewhat veiled, yet sonorously powerful and beautifully clarified tone" which is said to have marked Spohr's own playing remains the ideal which the student should strive to attain.

In addition to the Concerto, Op. 47, the "Lyric Scene," which remains Spohr's masterpiece, I regard as admirable, I might almost say indispensable study material (among the 17 concertos the composer wrote) his Second Concerto, in B minor; his Seventh Concerto, in E minor and, especially, his Ninth Concerto in D minor.**

CHAPTER VII.

HENRI VIEUXTEMPS.

Despite all the important services Vieuxtemps has rendered violin literature in general and the concert repertory in particular his achievements, especially in the last-mentioned direction, are not adequately recognized in our own day. It always should be borne in mind that although Vieuxtemps' (1820-1881) numerous individual pieces, including his seven concertos, were written from the standpoint of virtuoso effect, they were developed with far more care, and their musical values were far greater than was the case with most of the other music of this type produced in his time. In his scores,

---

** These three concertos appear in the editions I have revised for the house of Carl Fischer, Inc., New York.

as Wasiliewski truly says: "Vieuxtemps unquestionably strove
to raise the orchestral accompaniment of his concert pieces
from the low level of a mere accompaniment, and give them
a musically interesting form, based on a thoroughgoing thematic
development."

The trend toward absolute music after the model of
Beethoven, Mendelssohn and, later on, Brahms, so powerful
and universal during the past few decades was at the time
when young Vieuxtemps wrote his First Concerto, Op. 10, in
E major,* confined in Europe to certain very select and limited
musical circles.   In those days Paris lay under the spell of
the triumphs Meyerbeer had scored with his "Le Prophète"
and "Les Huguenots," triumphs which had greatly excited
the musical world.   Vieuxtemps did not escape this dominant
psychosis.   He treated his orchestra in the Meyerbeerian style,
using trumpets, tubas, kettle-drum and cymbals in his orchestral
accompaniments, something unheard of at the time in connection with the solo concerto,** especially in Paris, which was
then ultra-conservative.   Haydn, Mozart—Beethoven less
frequently—reigned on the concert stage; at times works by
Cherubini were heard.   The programmes played by the solo
artists were drawn from the existing classic repertoire, and from
the compositions of the individual virtuosos.   And into this
field young Vieuxtemps projected himself with an actual
symphonic concerto for violin, his Op. 10.

Henri Wieniawski told me—and what he said had been
told him by an actual eye- and ear-witness—that when Vieuxtemps made his début with the Concerto in question, at one
of the Symphony Concerts at the *Salle du Conservatoire*, and
the orchestra had finished playing the pompous Introduction
(it concludes with a general pause *before the entrance of the
solo violin)* that both public and orchestra broke out into a
frenzied salvo of applause, a tremendous tribute paid Vieuxtemps the *composer!*   And Vieuxtemps, at a later date, expressed his satisfaction at this homage paid him, adding that

---

* Henri Vieuxtemps. Concerto No. 1, in E major, Op. 10. Revised and edited
by Theodore Spiering. Carl Fischer, Inc., New York.

** Franz Liszt must be mentioned as an exception to this rule. His two piano
concertos were written during his Weimar period (1848-1861) contemporaneous with
that in which Vieuxtemps composed.

he regarded it as the highest praise ever accorded him during
his virtuoso career.

Where the solo violin enters in the first movement, Vieuxtemps, like Paganini (Concerto No. 1 D major), begins with
half notes, *forte*, *energico*, in playing which the student should
not overlook the accents:

especially those on the up-bow!

It should be taken in a very broad tempo, the *piano* melody
at measure nine from the beginning:

with much intimate feeling. The passage in triplets at letter
D, both the composer himself and Henri Wieniawski always
played at the *point* of the bow, *martelé*, which makes it sound
more beautiful than when it is played at the nut, where there
is always danger of forcing the tone.

At letter **E** the same passage, half a tone lower and *piano:*

should, on the contrary, be taken *spiccato*, with the middle of
the bow.

The Second Theme in B major (eleventh measure after
letter **E**) should be rendered very songfully, and hence with
much quietude and simplicity:

gradually developing to a tremendous climax at letter **F**.

At the *Più presto* I would advise the student in case he is the master of a good quick *staccato*,* first to practice the scale *legato*, slurring the notes, and when the left hand work is perfect, technically, then to attempt the same passage *staccato*, either ascending V or descending ⊓ . The latter usually is preferable, since the high notes respond, i. e., "speak" more readily at the point of the bow than in the middle.

The *Maestoso* succeeding the grand orchestral *tutti* should be played in free style, like a *Recitative*, during its first eight measures, at:

after which the *Maestoso* tempo once more comes into its own.

The following passage:

is one which I instance in order to advise the student against using too much pressure while playing it.

When playing the Concerto in public, an optional cut may be made in the orchestral *tutti*, *fortissimo*, from the eighth measure after letter **M** to four measures *before* the Cadenza. The Cadenza is free-form, must be played with freedom and independence and, for the reason already given, all *staccato* scales, so far as possible, should be played with the down-bow.

The Second Movement (Introduction: *Adagio*) is short and very melodious, and serves to introduce the very graceful "Rondo." In view of the brevity of the *Adagio* and its numerous thirty-second and sixty-fourth note passages, which *must not* sound hurried, a very slow tempo is in order, and to this end the two quarters (2/4) should each be divided into four sixteenths (4/16).

The Third Movement (Rondo: *Allegretto*) can be played properly only by those who control a rapid, equalized *staccato*.

For only a *staccato* of this type will do justice to the graceful character of the composition. After the short orchestral introduction, the solo violin enters as follows:

The above eleven B naturals determine the character of the entire Finale. The student should begin powerfully and slowly, retarding more and more, with a corresponding *diminuendo* in tone, up to *a tempo*, where the theme—played *piano* and in strict time—commences. Every individual tone must sound in unison at the nut, and be briefly and positively uttered.

The tempo is conditioned by the rapidity of the *staccato*, which must not be hurried. Strict rhythm and equality in the production of the *staccato* lend the piece its inherent charm. The entire Concerto is very long, too long, in fact, even when the last two movements only are played. Hence I would advise the following optional cut in this movement: from one measure before the *Più presto:* (p. 19 of Violin Score)

to one measure before letter **K**:

The succeeding passage should be taken *pianissimo*, and as lightly and rapidly as at all possible. After the orchestral *tutti* we then have an intermezzo "sung" on the G-string, whose first two measures are taken from the Introduction *(Adagio)*. Although the student will not find it indicated in the music, a broader tempo is decidedly called for here. At letter **L**, the composer indicates a *Poco animato:*

which (at letter **M**), leads over to the original a tempo of the "Rondo."

From the end of the fifteenth measure after letter **N** on:

I would advise a cut duplicating the cut already advocated, this time to one measure before letter **P**, i. e.:

playing the following passages very lightly and rapidly to the end.

In Vieuxtemps' Fourth Concerto in D minor, Op. 31,* which is the next outstanding concerto among the composer's seven, he has essayed to extend the concerto form. To the customary three movements he adds a fourth, a "Scherzo," which is a highly perfected composition as regards both feeling and rhythm. This movement, unfortunately, in most cases is sacrificed when the Concerto is played. The young virtuosos fear that the four movements will seem too long, so they drop the "Scherzo" and pass directly from the *Adagio religioso*

---

* Henri Vieuxtemps. Concerto No. 4 in D minor, Op. 31. Edited by August Wilhelmj. Carl Fischer, Inc., New York.

(Second Movement) to the Finale. The latter, it is true, contains some uncommonly brilliant moments; yet personally I prefer the "Scherzo." In the *Adagio religioso* the composer uses the harp, which enters with wellnigh magic effect. Only those whose ideas with regard to solo music are thoroughly antiquated will have anything but praise for the composer's merits in enriching and perfecting his orchestral accompaniment.

After a dramatically conceived orchestral prelude the solo violin sets in with a Recitative. In discussing the principles governing the presentation of the violin recitative in connection with the Bruch Concerto in D minor and Spohr's *Gesangsscene* (Eighth Concerto), I said that hints could be given regarding their practical observance though theoretically they cannot be detailed. The *character* of music to be played in the recitative style always determines its interpretation, and is the main point at issue. Whoever is able spiritually to grasp the conception expressed in the tonal language of the composition in question is sure to express it again so that the auditor will understand it.

In this particular Recitative it is important that the *first note* be sustained as long as possible, and with the utmost beauty of tone: the bow must seem to be endless on the string. The chords which follow should be played with great breadth until the player reaches the *Appassionato:*

140.

mf appassionato

where the tempo becomes somewhat more animated.

The Cadenza is conceived on broad, sweeping lines. The first chords should be taken slowly, the ones following in eighths, rather shortly, so that the intervening eighth-pause is perceptible. The arpeggio passages and the scale sequence at the end may be played as rapidly as is consistent with clear execution.

In the *Andante religioso* (Second Movement), the few measures of orchestral introduction at once supply the key to

the mood in which the composition is conceived. The entrance
of the solo violin:

is full of poetry, and must sound as though the tone were floating down from the skies. In accordance with its title—*Adagio
religioso*—the movement must be interpreted in a spirit of the
greatest reverence and with inner conviction. Yet it also contains dramatic moments such as that occurring six measures
before letter **E**:

which is maintained until the entrance of the harp in the
orchestra:

The interpretation of this *intrata*, marked by the greatest
serenity, demands the employ of a lovely, etherial quality of
tone by the solo violin.

The "Scherzo" *(Vivace)*, the neglected Third Movement
of this Concerto, is full of piquant charm. It sounds best when
played with the upper half of the bow, and its tempo is conditioned by a clear, perfected performance of the following
difficult passage:

which continues for twelve measures further. It must be taken
in the lightest kind of *staccato*, and played—I might almost
say—with absolutely *mechanical* evenness.

Some twenty measures after letter **H** occurs a chromatic scale in trills which the rapid tempo renders well nigh impossible of execution. In my own London edition of the work* I have altered it as follows:

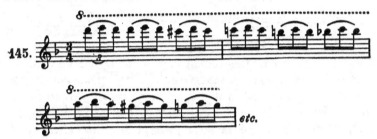

145.

The Trio of this "Scherzo," played *Meno mosso*, has a species of hunting theme; the solo violin first imitates two hunting horns (French horns minus valve) and later the clarinet. At letter **K** the hunting motive appears in the orchestra, and then reverts to the "Scherzo" proper by means of an extended *stringendo* and *crescendo*.

The Finale *(Allegro),* is introduced by a great orchestral prelude:

146.

The energetic character of the Principal Theme of this Finale reveals itself. It should be taken at the point of the bow as a *martelé-stroke* up to the *a tempo:*

147.

where the down-bow is prescribed for all the chords.

---

* Henri Vieuxtemps. Concerto No. 4, in D minor, Op. 31. Edited by Leopold Auer. B. Schott & Sons, London.

Naturally the sixteenth-note passage which follows, marked *leggierissimo*, should be played as indicated. After the orchestral *tutti* we have the Second Theme:

148.

Here I would advise the student to play somewhat more quietly and with gentle expressiveness for all that *piano* and *appassionato* are prescribed in the score, since these two indications may quite possibly be due to a printer's error in the original edition! at letter **G** we have a reprise of the First Theme as at the beginning.

Letter **S** leads on to the long triple stop chord sequence of diminished sevenths. Students who find that this passage does not "sound beautiful"—and this will include the majority—may use my London edition of the work aforementioned, where it has been altered; or they may simply drop the chords in question entirely, making a cut from one measure before the beginning:

149.

to four measures before the letter **T**:

150.

Among Vieuxtemps' concertos is still another* which, in my opinion emphatically deserves consideration, and which the artist and advanced student should know. This is the composer's Fifth Concerto in A minor, Op. 37. I always have wished to hear this Concerto in A minor presented by some great virtuoso on the concert stage, with orchestra accompaniment, but my wish has not been granted up to the present day. I myself played it in concert on two different occasions a long time ago—some forty to fifty years—in Holland, with

* Henri Vieuxtemps, Concerto No. 5, Op. 37, in A minor. Revised and edited by Theodore Spiering. Carl Fischer, Inc., New York.

Dutch symphony orchestras, and no longer have the faintest recollection of my impressions or those of my audiences.

In more recent years this work has been practically forgotten, and when one of the younger virtuosos is brave enough to play it in public, which very seldom happens, the critics turn up their noses, talk of "shallow and valueless music, empty phrases merely intended to supply an excuse for the demonstration of technical superiority," etc.

Hence the young artist withdraws in confusion, and plays Johann Sebastian Bach's Concerto in E major, or Vivaldi's Concerto in A minor at his next recital. It goes without saying that both these last-mentioned works contain more absolute music, the Vivaldi Concerto** (in the Tivadar Nachez edition) in particular.

Whether the great body of concertgoers would prefer to them the Vieuxtemps Concerto which, after all, contains some very beautiful violin music, is something which could not well be determined without a vote. Yet when the Vieuxtemps Concerto in A minor is played as its composer *meant* it to be played, it will not fail to impress the majority of its auditors. For it is *not* a work made up of empty externals, but rather one which shows the violin at its best, qualitatively. And it has the merit of conciseness: it consists of two rather extended movements, connected by a brilliant Cadenza which leads over to a short final Coda composed of passages from the First Movement.

In this First Movement (*Allegro non troppo*) the solo violin begins with a brief Introduction, recitative in style, and in a quiet tempo which soon, however, as the composer's indications show, grows more animated; and at No. 4 a brief theme enters, leading over by means of scales and passages to No. 5:

151.

which is the continuation of the theme in question. From the

** Antonio Vivaldi, Concerto in A minor. Revised and edited by Tivadar Nachez. Carl Fischer, Inc., New York.

very start of the movement as well as in the passages which
follow, a decidedly quiet tempo is advisable.

At No. 7 is introduced the Second Theme:

which, as regards its melodic invention and development, must
be counted among the Concerto's best movements. It is
repeated by the orchestra while the solo violin brings forward
broken chords and a specifically *détaché* passage in Vieuxtemps' most characteristic manner. The orchestral *tutti* in C
major presents a motive borrowed from the Introduction; and
the same motive also supplies the continuation of the First
Movement in the solo violin part.

From Nos. 12 to 14 we have inversions and extension of the
songful motive at No. 7. The *martelé* passage which follows:

is an admirable study for both hands, especially the right.

With regard to the two optional Cadenzas my own preference inclines to No. 2; which by no means implies a vote of
no confidence in No. 1. Both are admirable in invention, and
each in connection with the remainder of the work forms a
harmonious unit. With regard to the interpretation of
Cadenzas no authoritative rules exist. As in the case of the
Recitative, a sense of style, good taste and musical experience
are the factors which must point the way for the player.

The Second Movement *(Adagio)*, should be taken very slowly and its quarters divided into eighths. It introduces a folk song (I believe it is a Belgian melody entitled, *Où peut-on être mieux que dans sa patrie)*:

which appears at No. 17, and gradually developing with a great *stretto*, reaches its climax at No. 20. It is immediately followed by the *Allegro con fuoco*, with the close.

Aside from these three concertos which we have discussed, two additional Vieuxtemps' concertos have appeared in print. One is the Second Concerto in F sharp minor,* whose technical utility has won grateful recognition; the other the Third Concerto, in A major,† less happily inspired. Yet its *Adagio* is a good study for tone development; and its last movement offers an abundance of *staccato* passages for those who desire to perfect themselves in this bowing.

Among the composer's many other compositions with piano accompaniment, I might mention his "Ballade and Polonaise," an interesting number which still occasionally turns up on the recital programme; the "Fantaisie Appassionato,"** the "Fantaisie Caprice," the "Rêverie" (valuable as a tone study), and the graceful little "Rondino," each of which in its own way may be recommended as useful teaching material.

* Henri Vieuxtemps, Concerto No. 2, in F sharp minor. Revised and edited by Leopold Auer. Carl Fischer, Inc., New York.

† Henri Vieuxtemps, Concerto No. 3, in A major. Revised and edited by Leopold Auer. B. Schott & Sons, London.

** Henri Vieuxtemps, "Fantaisie Appassionato." Revised and edited by Leopold Auer. B. Schott & Sons, London.

Chapter VIII.

HENRI WIENIAWSKI.

The compositions of Henri Wieniawski (1835-1880) all are brilliant and written with an eye to virtuoso effect, and his two concertos, his "Légende" and the "Mazourkas," especially, maintain their place as favorite repertoire numbers in concert and recital. Wieniawski's Concerto No. 1, in F sharp minor, Op. 14,* which the composer wrote while still a young virtuoso, already shows the lion's claws. It is conventional only in form. Otherwise this concerto, especially in its first movement with its heroic Principal Theme in tenths, and also in the passages at letter **C**, proves to be the creation of a young iconoclast who seizes every opportunity to reveal his exceptionally brilliant technical powers.

After the passage-work which precedes it, the songful Second Theme in A major:

makes all the more effective an impression. After letter **D** we find a most characteristic passage, formed of a number of sequential chords:

interrupted by scales in thirds and octaves, which offer both the left hand and the right wrist grateful material for perfection exercises. The Cadenza—in spite of the *staccato* and *spiccato* passages which characterize the theme and its development—is conceived in the pathetic style, and should so be played. The full and detailed manner in which the Cadenza

---

* Henri Wieniawski, Concerto No. 1, in F sharp minor, Op. 14. Edited and revised by Leopold Auer. Carl Fischer, Inc., New York.

(and for that matter the entire concerto) has been provided
with expression marks practically precludes any possibility of
misunderstanding the composer's wishes and intentions, if the
student carefully observe them.

If the Concerto in F sharp minor does not, perhaps, cor-
respond to the musical ideals of the present day, it is, nevertheless, a noteworthy individual contribution to violin literature
and a valuable musical study of the period which followed
upon the death of Paganini and of Ernst.

The Second Movement, "Preghiera" *(Larghetto)*, does not
call for extended consideration. It is a "Prayer," very short,
and very simply conceived which, in addition to a warm, beautiful tone, demands for its proper interpretation the inward
conviction of the believer whose invocation rises to the skies
with full sincerity and faith.

The Third Movement, "Rondo" *(Allegro giocoso)* has a
theme which supplies a welcome exercise in the short, dotted
martelé stroke. The stroke should come from the wrist; yet
if the development of a more powerful tone seem desirable,
the student will do well to use the forearm in connection with
the wrist. He will be able to judge by the *quality* of the tone
he produces how far and to which degree the forearm may
be brought into action in order to preserve intact the tonal
beauty of the bowing.

At the *Maggiore* after letter **Q** appears the Second Theme:

157.

which should be played with much warmth; and at letter **R**
it repeats on the G-string, an octave lower; while later, in the
orchestra, it serves as a foundation for the graceful variations
of the solo violin. The Coda marked Finale:

158.

quite aside from its melodic content, is an admirable exercise
for the short *détaché* and may be played, as preferred, in the
middle or at the point of the bow. It might be mentioned, in
addition, that the prescribed *ben ritmico* may be secured by an
exact marking of the accent on each triplet.

Henri Wieniawski's Concerto No. 2, in D minor, Op. 22,*
is a work of a later period, and seems to have been written
under the influence of Gounod, Saint-Saëns and, perhaps, Lalo.
As regards its voice leading, its form and its orchestration—
which last has been handled with admirable good taste and
expert knowledge—it shows the composer intended to write
not merely a virtuoso composition for the violin, but to produce
as well an interesting musical creation. The great success of
this concerto, which is played by practically *all* the great
virtuosos of our time, compares only with that achieved by
Saint-Saëns' Concerto in B minor and Lalo's "Symphonie
espagnole."   (In making this comparison I except, of course,
the three violin super-concertos, those of Beethoven, Mendelssohn and Brahms.)   The Wieniawski Concerto in D minor
to this day sounds as fresh and spontaneous as it did when the
composer first played it in public fifty-five years ago.

The First Movement is the lyric creation of an artist striv-
ing to realize lofty aims; one cannot help but feel that the
composer reveals his feelings with all sincerity, and that he does
not shrink from expressing the most exalted outbursts of passion. The initial tempo, as indicated by the composer, is
Allegro moderato. Wieniawski himself played this first movement rather quietly, *more moderato than Allegro*, which is
justified by the character of his motives, and the indication
Dolce, ma sotto voce. This mood is maintained until, shortly
before the passage in D minor, the First Theme concludes with
the *fortissimo* section in octaves (with its preceding *crescendo)*
and the passage in D minor in question:

159.   *etc.*

p molto legato e tranquillo

---

* Henri Wieniawski, Concerto No. 2, in D minor, Op. 22. Carl Fischer, Inc.,
New York.

appears and later, through an *Appassionato:*

f appassionato

which is a transformation of the First Theme.

The triplet:

that occurs in it sounds like an anticipation of the subsequent Second Theme, one which is all the more effective because of its unpretentious simplicity:

p semplice

Then follows the passage in triplets:

which Wieniawski, when he played it, began at the *point* of the bow, as a *martelé,* playing the following measures *détaché,* and at the return of the First Theme (see Example given) reverted to the *martelé* once more. In the passage following:

f

the student should use a *détaché* with the lower part of the bow, and sharply emphasize the notes which are marked for accentuation.

The Second Movement, "Romance," is marked *Andante non troppo,* and the phrase sums up all that need be said regarding it. It is a song to be sung in a way which will make us forget the instrument.

The Third Movement, "à la Zingara," is marked *Allegro moderato*. We have mentioned in connection with the First Movement, which bears the same tempo indication, that in its case a *moderate tempo*, not a real *Allegro* is more in keeping with the music. For this Third Movement I would like to suggest the *exact contrary:* more *Allegro* and less *moderato*. With regard to the manner of playing I would recommend a partial *spiccato* where a *piano* is indicated, as at the beginning; and a *détaché* when the music calls for an employ of greater power, as at the *crescendos* and *fortes*. With the appearance of the Second Theme of the First Movement, which in this Third Movement also forms the song-motive:

the mood grows somewhat quieter while later, at the *Molto appassionato*, the player should carry on with the maximum of tone and urgency and *without* stop until the last note has been played.

At D major:

play with much energy and strictly in time. Before the close there occurs a *Brilliante con fuoco:*

which invites playing in a more rapid tempo. If the student follows this impulse, however, he will sacrifice the clarity and accuracy of the succeeding passage in sixteenth-notes.

In addition to the two concertos we have just discussed, Wieniawski wrote a "Fantasy on Motives from Gounod's Faust," which is a notable favorite in the concert repertoire, and suggests Liszt's genial Fantasy on themes from Mozart's "Don Giovanni,,; and a number of shorter compositions. Among the latter I might call special attention to the "Légende," the two "Polonaises," respectively in D and A major, the "Scherzo-Tarantelle" and the "Souvenir de Moscou." These four numbers last-mentioned, together with the Faust Fantasy, may be seen to this day on the programmes of the majority of concert violinists. Last, but not least, Wieniawski wrote some exceedingly piquant "Mazurkas" which, seeing that he was a native pole, came straight from the heart. All these compositions are virtuoso pieces, pure and simple, though they deserve to be ranked among the best of their type.

It is very difficult to describe these pieces in detail. Every experienced player will interpret them according to his own conception, if he possess the technique essential to play them and has absorbed their individual nature and character. The student should consult his teacher with regard to interpretation, while at the same time developing his own taste and concept by hearing famous artists play them. In this instance we have no traditions, beauty alone supplies the determinant.

With regard to the "Polonaises," I would like to call the student's attention to the fact that this dance-form has a pompous, festival character. At courts of the Russian czars and the Prussian kings the Polonaise, on ceremonial occasions, opened the ball. The monarch in question—and this applied to the Polish court as well—led out one of the first ladies of the land, and was followed by princes, princesses and his noble guests or, to use the customary phrase, "those whose attendance at Court had been commanded." Each cavalier held his lady's hand and the dance was not danced, but "stepped" in slow, solemnly rhythmic movement.

It is with regret that I often hear Wieniawski's two "Polonaises" in the concert hall as well as in the studio, played with exaggerated haste and *rubatissimo*. This applies especially to the "Polonaise" in D major and, as I have just made clear, is contrary to its historic character and the composer's intentions. This I know because I repeatedly heard Wieniawski play both his "Polonaises" in the circle of his intimate friends and on the concert stage.

I by no means claim that the "Polonaises" should be played on the concert stage in the unvaried solemn tempo of the royal ball room. The rhythm of the principle theme, however, should awaken in the auditor the feeling of a festival "pacing off" of the dance, and this was evidently the composer's intention, else he would not have called these compositions "Polonaises."

CHAPTER IX.

JOACHIM AND ERNST.

Of Joseph Joachim's three violin concertos, his Concerto in D minor, in the Hungarian Style, Op. 11,* is the most important, and the meaning of its title *must be accepted literally*. The composer calls it a "Concerto in the Hungarian Style," i. e., *not* one built up on Hungarian folk-themes. The themes are original ones by Joachim, though they have the pronounced Hungarian character which, seeing that Joachim (1831-1907) was a Hungarian born, sounded on his inner ear and echoed in his heart.

I am the only still surviving pupil of Joachim who has studied the "Hungarian Concerto" with the master himself, and I mention the fact in order to give greater weight to my considerations. The Concerto is one hardly ever found on the programmes of contemporary violin virtuosos, and this discrimination against it is most unjust since owing to its interesting themes and its perfected classic form, it is a work well worthy of consideration. As study material for the student violinist who wishes to attain the highest degree of development it is invaluable, and this is due largely to the pronounced technical individuality of the first two movements.

After the long orchestra prelude which presents all the principal and secondary themes of the work, the solo violin

---

* Joseph Joachim, *Konzert in ungarischer Weise* in D moll, Op. 11. Original edition, Breitkopf & Hartel, Leipsic.

commences with a dreamy introduction which soon—in a most
original passage marked *Largamente*—rushes downward like
some furious mountain torrent, and gradually growing more
subdued, leads to the Principal Theme:

a theme which should be sung on the instrument with the most
intimate feeling and a beautiful tone.

At letter **C** we meet one of those passages whose individuality already has been stressed. It calls for a very light wrist-
action across the strings. It soon is followed by the Second
Theme:

prepared by a few measures in the orchestra; and developed
by the solo violin and the orchestra in alternation, with a
stretto which drives forward with ever greater urgency to cul-
minate in the passionate climax:

which leads to the *fortissimo* entrance of the orchestra.

At letter **F** commences a short thematic working-out which, after a series of brilliant passages, reintroduces the First Theme. Noteworthy is the short phrase marked *piangente:*

which should be played in a plaintive manner—the "tears" for which the composer calls actually trembling in the violin-tone—and the subsequent original passage in octaves on the chromatic scale. The Cadenza—it should be played as quietly and serenely as possible—demonstrates the composer's authority inasmuch as it, together with the closing measures, forms the technical climacteric point of the First Movement.

The Second Movement, the "Romanza" is a song *in the Hungarian style,* and *not* a Hungarian song. Joachim did not follow the example of Franz Liszt who utilized folk-songs and national dances in such a genial way in his "Hungarian Rhapsodies." Joachim created independently of both. He "felt" in a Hungarian manner, and gave this inner feeling tonal expression in his themes.

The two quarters indicated (2/4) should be divided into four rather slow eighths, for the singable quality of the "Romanza" will be the gainer thereby. The second section, *Con Fuoco:*

demands a more movemented tempo up to the moment when the theme appears in the orchestra and the solo violin weaves its music about it in a most original way.*

---

* These decorative figures imitate the Hungarian Gipsy *simbalon*—an instrument with steel strings which are struck by two wooden-hammers with felt covered heads.

A Più moto, poco Allegretto:

174.

p

varies the tempo until the following passage is reached:

175.

p espressivo

and this passage is one which should be played as warmly and intimately as possible, the two holds, in accordance with this mood, being decidedly long sustained. The *Allegretto* which follows should be taken rather softly, and the tone should be allowed to die away *very quietly* in the four concluding measures.

The Third Movement, "Finale alla Zingara" is an *Allegro* which, in spite of the fact that it is in minor, justifies a very animated tempo. For the *sempre staccato* must be played in the sense of a *spiccato*, which at the *crescendi* and *rinforzandi* merges into a *détaché*.

Two measures after letter **C** appears the Second Theme:

176.

p   *ff*

to be played strictly in time, at the nut, and stressing the contrast between *piano* and *forte*. Succeeding letter **D** comes the great orchestral *tutti*, after which a new theme makes its appearance:

177.

p

This theme should be played in a somewhat less animated tempo and in a very songful manner.

In view of the fact that this movement is of quite extraordinary length, and that it is preceded by two other extended movements, I would advise the following cut in the event of public performance: Skip from the last measure of letter **D** to the first measure of letter **G**. The *Presto* indicated before the close should also be taken very rapidly, and more tempestuously the nearer the player approaches the end.

The Concerto in F sharp minor, Op. 23,* by Heinrich Wilhelm Ernst (1814-1865) makes the very highest demands on the technique of both hands and together with the composer's other, not very numerous works, supplies one of the most important factors in the higher development of a violin left-hand technique. Ernst was a contemporary of Paganini. He was influenced by that epoch-making genius and even, in a measure, imitated him. Yet he did not entirely sacrifice his own originality and independence. His compositions, though they all pay tribute to the trend of his age toward virtuosity, are by no means commonplace.

The cantabile portion of this concerto is extremely rich, elaborate and beautiful, and decidedly heightens the value of the composition. It would be unjust to regard the work as one which aims only at external effect; in part, to be sure, it represents no more than technical violinistic "apparatus," mechanical scaffolding; but its major portion, owing to its genuine musical content, and the manner in which its themes—in the orchestra as well as in the violin solo part—have been developed, gives it a place among the more distinguished works of its kind written for the instrument.

The First Theme (letter **B**), after the five measures of introduction, is heroic in character, and this fact must be borne in mind in the attack, which should be made with breadth and energy and with a noble tone. At the *Con molto espressione:* (between letters **C** and **D**).

178.

play with great warmth; and accentuate the octave triplets which follow in a very decided manner. Ten measures after

---

* H. W. Ernst, Concerto in F sharp minor. Revised and edited by Leopold Auer. Carl Fischer, Inc., New York.

letter **F** we encounter the Second Principal Theme; and at
letter **G** a very graceful variation which—in spite of the tenths
in the highest positions and its other technical difficulties—
should be played so that it sounds very light and airy until
(at letter **H**) a greater degree of passion must be expressed.

After a reminiscence of the First Principal Theme at letter
L, we reach (letter **M**) an orchestral passage of great lyric
beauty, above which the solo violin soars in an ascending flight:

which passage together with the solo melody that follows
should be played as expressively as possible to form a contrast
to the *Resoluto, forte,* at letter **N**.

At letter **O** we meet a new *cantabile* theme:

which is repeated by the orchestra while the solo violin sus-
tains the trill on A, at the same time playing against it two
brilliant scales. These last must be played strictly in time in
order not to diminish the effect of the orchestral melody. The
Quasi recitativo before letter **V** should be taken in a very sustained manner, and this also applies to the *Lento* which follows.

The octave passage which occurs four measures after the
letter **W** is very original: it begins *piano* (this *piano* is missing
in my edition!) and carries its octave-sequence through a
powerful *crescendo* built up on an organ-point on **C** sharp to
the second Principal Theme in F sharp major:

in order to pass later to the *Allegro molto,* played at double
the speed of the preceding tempo. Much depends when play-

ing Ernst, on giving the *musical* "high moments" in his compositions their proper value and effect, and this is as true of the Concerto in F sharp minor as it is of his shorter pieces.

Two works by Ernst—once his concerto has been considered—stand out: his "Otello,"* a "Fantaisie brilliant" on themes from Rossini's opera, and his "Elégie." Of these the "Elégie" is the more popular, while the "Otello" Fantasy is, perhaps, the most important. Even though as a concert program number it does not conform to the spirit of our age, it remains a work with a very valid claim to consideration from the standpoint of perfection in finger technique. Taken as a whole, the "Otello" Fantasy is a *lyric* work, and should be played with this fact in mind.

The Introduction is an original contribution on the part of Ernst and musically, too, shows a fine quality of invention. The Cadenza (letter **B**) which leads over to the march-theme may be recommended as an excellent daily finger-exercise. At letter **D** we have the "March" upon whose theme the three variations, each very characteristic in its own way, have been constructed. This march-theme should be played in genuine military march time, and the chords as well as the double-stops it contains must not be allowed to interfere with the observance of this strict military march rhythm.

The First Variation introduces passages in thirds, sixths and tenths in the most varied positions. Every section of this variation should be repeated, the first time playing it *forte*, with a broad *détaché* stroke, and the second time *piano*, as follows:

using the middle of the bow and taking the two *staccato* notes with a light bow from the wrist. The second section of the

---

* H. W. Ernst, "Otello," "Fantaisie brilliante." Revised and edited by Arno Hilf. Carl Fischer, Inc., New York.

variation should be played in the same way as the first, with
the exception that the passage in octaves marked *crescendo:*

183.

on *both occasions* be played with a broad *détaché* bowing and
a large tone.

The Second Variation offers an admirable exercise in chords
combined with leaps to the high E:

184.

The E, played as a harmonic note, must sound full and round
in tone, somewhat more than half the bow being used; and
the whole variation should be taken at a *very moderate* tempo
and played with a clear, beautiful tone quality. The *Andante*
at letter **B** is one of the loveliest arias with which Rossini has
enriched the older Italian operatic repertoire. It expresses,
in accordance with his text, the scene in Desdemona's bed-
chamber.* The tragic victim of marital jealousy is alarmed
by the presentiment of her coming death and this torturing
anticipation should be expressed in every note of the violin aria.
Ernst has caught and held in his violin working-out all the
tragic truth and beauty of Desdemona's presentiment, and this
mood is maintained in his music until letter **D** is reached, where
the technical element and the Cadenza which follows once
more occupy the foreground of interest.

The Third Variation is probably the most difficult of the
three. It is a *legato* study with *arpeggios* and leaps in tenths.

* It is the aria *Desdemona* sings in Act IV of the opera, while she is awaiting
death at Otello's hands. The score first was heard in 1816, long before the advent of
"verism," when the public was not yet hardened to the slaughter of operatic heroines
with every refinement of brutality. As in the "movies" to-day, operatic audiences
liked tragedies to have a "happy ending." So when "Otello" was given in Rome for
the first time the ending was changed to win public favor. When Otello was about
to throttle Desdemona a duet was interpolated. Desdemona cried: "What would you
do, unhappy man? I am innocent!" "Is this the very truth?" asked the Moor. And
when Desdemona swore it was, he seized her hand and both stepping up to the foot-
lights, sang a jolly *Allegro* of reconciliation from some other Rossini score so that
every one could go home happy.

A free and flexible wrist movement across the strings and carrying out changes in position in an unnoticeable manner are essential in order to secure the desired tonal effects in this variation. At letter **B** the songful theme of the Introduction returns. At letter **C**:

a light, flying *staccato* is in order. This is a very graceful passage, with a more serious turn of expression in the four measures, *crescendo* to *fortissimo*—before the *Poco più lento*:

and the last measure in octaves, four measures before the close:

may be played with greater ease and surety if fingered octaves are used.

Aside from the Concerto in F sharp minor and the "Fantasie brilliante" on themes from Rossini's "Otello," already considered, Ernst also wrote a Concertino in D major,* "Airs Variés sur des Thèmes Hongrois" and "Six Caprices for Solo Violin,"** dedicated to distinguished colleagues of his own day—Joachim, Vieuxtemps, Laub, Bazzini, Sainton and Josef Hellmesberger. These études, though their musical value is mediocre, contain much excellent study material. Unfortunately they are useful only to students when the latter have

---

* H. W. Ernst. Concertino in D major. Revised and edited by Leopold Auer. G. Schirmer, Inc., New York.

** H. W. Ernst. "Six Caprices for Solo Violin." Revised and edited by Leopold Auer. G. Schirmer, Inc., New York.

large hands and long fingers to enable them to overcome their difficulties. This, however, now and again happens to be the case.

In the same category belongs the transcription of Schubert's wonderful ballad, "The Erlking." It is wellnigh impossible for the four strings of the violin, minus an orchestra or a piano accompaniment, to do justice to the highly dramatic character of "The Erlking." Hence the work is practically never heard on the concert stage. It is essentially a technical étude, and belongs in the studio.

Two other compositions by the same composer date from the Romantic period, the middle of the nineteenth century. These are the "Elégie," which in its day lured many a tear from sentimental feminine eyes; and the "Carneval de Venise," a "War-horse" of antiquated virtuosity. Both compositions vanished from the concert stage more than fifty years ago.

CHAPTER X.

THE THREE MASTER-CONCERTOS OF VIOLIN LITERATURE.

(Beethoven, Mendelssohn, Brahms)

Though the choice of Beethoven's (1809), Mendelssohn's (1844) and Brahms' (1879) concertos as the three outstanding "master concertos" written for the violin is, of course, an individual one and represents primarily my own conviction, I believe it is one I share with the majority of violinists. I also have preferred to consider them together in view of the fact that the considerations advanced in my "Introduction" anent the first essentials of an interpretation which reveals the soul of the composer's music, especially the principle of the variation of effect, are the more important the greater the work in question, and apply especially to these three super-concertos.

Let us consider Beethoven's Violin Concerto,* for example. At its very beginning the composer has set down: *Allegro, ma*

---

* Beethoven, Violin Concerto in D major. Revised and edited by Leopold Auer. Carl Fischer, Inc., New York.

non troppo, without any further indications of tempo. After
the orchestra has completed the exposition of the First Theme:

188.

the Second Theme:

189.

and the Secondary Themes.

190.

the solo voice enters on the dominant with a Cadenza which
leads over to the First or Principal Theme. Beethoven makes
a rhythmic division of this entrance of the solo voice into
measures, without using the phrase *a piacere* or the word
"Cadenza." And yet the fact is that he *meant* to use either
the one or the other. This is indicated by the three short
dominant chords in the orchestra:

190 ½

and the six-measure pause preceding the entrance of the
Principal Theme in the solo violin part.

191.

All tempo indications are missing at the introduction of the
other themes. Does this mean that the entire First Movement,
from beginning to end, is to be played in the same tempo,
Allegro, ma non troppo? I am very much inclined to doubt
it, and invariably advise my pupils to *modify* their tempos in

accordance with the *character* of the themes themselves without, however, exaggerating such modifications: For example:

From this point on, after the lyric beginning of the First
Movement, the tempo should be very energetic and movemented up to the entrance of the Second Theme in A major,
in the orchestra:

which again quietly returns to the tempo of the beginning.
One of the most important rules, one which I myself have
always observed and now teach, is to make a distinction in
expression when playing *major* and *minor* themes. Usually
music which moves in a minor key is more contemplative, lyric
or dreamy, especially when it serves as a contrast to a leading
motive in a major key.

Thus, in Beethoven's Violin Concerto the G minor Theme
at letter **E**:

cannot be played in too quiet and intimate a manner. When
the Principal Theme, on the other hand, is in minor, as in
the First Movement of Mendelssohn's Violin Concerto,* with
an *Allegro molto appassionato* indicated at the beginning, the

---

* Mendelssohn, Violin Concerto, Op. 64. Revised and edited by Leopold Auer.
Carl Fischer, Inc., New York.

"passionate" character must be maintained until the soft, singing theme in G major:

has been reached; and this theme, of course, must be played in a very much quieter manner until the *appassionato* tempo once more begins with the entrance of the Principal Theme in G major:

After the Cadenza the lyric theme now is repeated in the fundamental key of E minor with the following extension:

These three measures often are played in the tempo indicated for the beginning of the First Movement. To my thinking the composer could not have intended them to be so played since the extension is a continuation of his second, his lyric theme.

    Reverting to the Beethoven Concerto, I should like to remark that after the Cadenza* in the First Movement, with its tempestuous passages in thirds—or in the octaves or tenths with which most virtuosos overburden their Cadenzas—the entrance of the Second Principal Theme:

should be played with as great tranquility as possible, and that this tranquil mood endures up to four measures before the end,

---

* A number of Cadenzas have been composed for the Beethoven Concerto, beginning with that by Joachim and ending with my own, the former published by Simrock, Berlin; the latter by Carl Fischer, Inc., New York.

when an *accellerando*, natural and obvious, even though it be
not indicated, should be observed in order to make it possible
for the player to attack the *Tempo primo*, the *Allegro, ma
non troppo*, as at the beginning, and to conclude the First
Movement as it began, energetically, yet without overspeeding,
I must again repeat that Beethoven does not indicate any
change of tempo, and that these observations of mine regarding the modification of the tempos he has indicated spring from
my own feeling and the aesthetic laws of music itself, and do
not pretend to be laid down as authoritative for every other
player.

The Second Movement, *Larghetto*, begins with the wonderful theme in G:

presented by the string quartet of the orchestra, the graceful,
poetic figuration of the solo violin floating above it.   It is one
of Beethoven's loveliest inspirations.   After a short original
Cadenza we meet with the Second Theme:

also in G major, which should be played *very slowly*, in same
tempo (Larghetto) as the beginning of the movement, or even
slower, and should at no time depart from its proper dreamy
character.   It draws to a close ever more softly, ever more
slowly, to die away in an expiring breath of tone.   With the
ff orchestral *tutti* on the dominant chord of D Major, we
awake to new life, and an *ad libitum* Cadenza leads us over
to the Third Movement, the *Rondo Allegro*.

I must confess that whenever I have heard the Beethoven
Concerto played by others, or when I have played it myself,
I have deeply regretted the fact that the *Larghetto* did not
end on the tonic, with a *pp*—it would have seemed like a
release, an escape from the intolerable oppression which weighs
one down!   Yet Beethoven felt this differently.   With his

brusque *ff* entrance of the orchestra he no doubt intended *suddenly* to carry the dreaming listener to new heights by sheer force.

The *Rondo Allegro*, in my opinion, should have been qualified by the adjective *energico*, for this is practically demanded by the Principal Theme (one might call it the "Hunting Theme") at the beginning, in contrast to the Second Theme. The secondary theme too:

retains the same energetic character until the Third Theme in G minor, prepared by an extended *diminuendo*, and played more quietly, *p, dolce:*

enters, in whose further development the splendid theme in B major, *espressivo*—naturally taken in a somewhat quieter tempo—with a lightly flowing variation and a preparatory *crescendo* to the *ff*, leads up to the Principal ("Hunting") Theme.

Succeeding the Cadenza we still have an inspired, indescribably beautiful modulation on the trill *(forte):*

after the A flat section we have the brilliant Coda, *ff*, which carries us to the close.

With regard to the Mendelssohn Concerto in E minor, I might add that its beginning, in spite of the indication *Molto appassionato*, which shows it should be played in a passionate,

---

* The *p dolce*, together with the preceding *diminuendo*, the *più p* and the *pp*, represents one of the most important details of shading in the Final Movement.

movemented fashion, *must be played piano* in order to make possible the working-up of the great *crescendo* leading up to the *forte:*

The greatest attention should be paid to the tone graduations and changes of tempo before the end of the First Movement:

and the *Sempre più,* the *presto* and the *prestissimo* also should be exactly observed.

The Second Movement, the *Andante,* is held in the lyric vein. It should be played very calmly and yet without any dragging. Beginning with the Second Theme:

the music assumes an agitated character, and in its development this mood reaches its climax at:

only to revert to its original calm and quiet. Then, in a continuing *diminuendo,* the calmly flowing figure of the solo violin again comes to the fore and leads over to the Principal Theme.

The *Allegretto non troppo* is of major importance in this work. It should be played rather quietly and with rather melancholy expressiveness as an introduction to the titillating, genial third movement, the *Allegro molto vivace.* This last movement is a typically Mendelssohnian composition. To this day (1925), it remains unequalled in originality of invention

in the violin repertory. At the beginning the composer has
written *Piano scherzoso:*

and *pianissimo leggiero* at the entrance of the Principal Theme:

Most students simply *ignore* this valuable interpretative
indication which Mendelssohn has prescribed. The last
eighth-note, A, with the pause, in the passage coming three
times in the measures preceding the beginning of the Principal
Theme is—contrary to the composer's indication—held as
though it were a quarter-note:

so that it completely destroys the aesthetic charm of the succeeding theme. I have heard the latter played in the concert
hall by virtuosos of recognized fame in a very clumsy manner,
inasmuch as they used *nearly half the bow* for the five *staccato*
notes: (see Ex. 209)

Sarasate somewhat exaggerated the tempo, yet every note he
played was full of magic poesy whenever it was at all possible
for the orchestra to follow him, and to avoid drowning him
out in the sixteenth-note passages:

Henri Wieniawski in the heydey of his career was accounted
the best interpreter of the Mendessohn Concerto owing to his
passionate temperament, which stood him in good stead, especially in the First Momevent. He played the last movement

in a *moderate* tempo and employed a light, fragrant *staccato;* which he used in a masterly manner throughout the entire movement. The medial passage which leads back to the Principal Theme:

Wieniawski always played strictly in time, *doubling* every eighth-note, so that the whole passage seemed to sparkle forth in an ascending *staccato* of sixteenth-notes like an electric spray, and the close in particular:

in descending *staccati*, made an enchanting impression because of the strict rhythm and the beautiful tone of the *staccato* itself.

A Third concerto, the Brahms Concerto in D,* belongs to the same category with the two already considered. In view of its intrinsic value—I beg the reader to remember that I am expressing only my own personal opinion in this connection—it is, after the concertos of Beethoven and Mendelssohn, the most important work in the entire literature of the violin. If I were to attempt to estimate the values of these three master works individually, I would go so far as to say that the Beethoven Concerto can boast the most beautiful Second Movement in its *Larghetto;* the Mendelssohn Concerto the most inspired Third Movement in its *Allegro molto vivace;* and the Brahms Concerto the most grandly planned First Movement in its *Allegro non troppo.*

* Johannes Brahms, Concerto for Violin in D, Op. 77. Revised and edited by Leopold Auer. Carl Fischer, Inc., New York.

It is written in the same key used by Beethoven and after
the orchestra has completed its exposition of the leading themes,
the solo violin begins with a passionately ascending D minor
scale in *forte*, based upon the Main Theme, and then flings
itself tempestuously down-hill like a mountain torrent until,
after long hesitation, an extended *diminuendo*—always on the
organ-point D—allows it to pass calmly over into the continu-
ously flowing figure:

while triplets (*espressivo*):

on the chord of the fourth-sixth, slowly lead back again to the
Principal Theme:

As a contrast we have the energetic violin theme:

The singing theme:

is magnificent and is repeated by the clarinet while the solo
violin offers a most engaging figure:

as a variant. Brahms' indication is *tranquillo*, in addition to
piano, and he also indicates various other shades of expression
—*tranquillo grazioso, leggiero, ma expressivo, etc.*—to show
how concerned he was that this passage for the solo violin be
properly interpreted.   Just *how* all the composer's wishes in
this respect are to be complied with must be left to the musical
sensibility of the individual performer.

After the customary Cadenza (at least half-a-dozen written
for this Concerto have appeared in print, among them Joachim's
Cadenza, one by Hugo Heermann and two I myself have
written) the Principal Theme, played *very quietly* and *dolce*
reappears, and the movement ends with an energetic and brilliant *Animato*.

The Second Movement, *Adagio*, begins with a lovely solo
for the oboe; and later the solo violin makes its entrance with
the same wonderful melody which it varies.   The second
section of the Middle Movement, *Più largamente:*

should be played *even more slowly* than the *First Theme*, and
with the very utmost warmth of expression.   Later we have
the variation:

in which the oboe and the flute alternately play the Principal
Theme, to which the solo violinist must adapt the figure in
sextolets above presented.   With the Coda:

perhaps the most affecting and moving moment of the whole
Concerto—the Second Movement comes to an end.

The composer has set down the tempo of the Third Movement as *Allegro giocoso, ma non troppo*, that is to say, "mer-

rily, yet not too animated." In my own edition of the Brahms'
Concerto I demand much energy and frequent accentuation
of the Principal Theme, which has a vaguely Hungarian
character. Unfortunately, this movement has no "singing"
theme to serve as a contrast. For this reason I have provided
the theme in three-quarter time:

with the indication *Meno mosso*, the more so since Brahms,
two measures further on:

writes *teneramente*—i. e., tenderly, delicately, a *dolce* somewhat infused with passion. This *Meno mosso* lasts until the
accelerando of the *Tempo primo* is reached; and the *Largamente* too, which follows later:

must be played with sustained calmness for the reason already
mentioned until the *energicamente* which the composer demands:

has been reached, and which by means of a short Cadenza
leads us to the *Poco più presto*. This last is provided with
the indication *ben marcato*, but in spite of the fact I advise
my pupils to play it very joyously and *molto leggiero*—as a
contrast to the Principal Theme up to the *Poco a poco
ritenuto:* two measures before the end of the movement the
composer calls for an energetic *a tempo*.

CHAPTER XI.

THE BRUCH CONCERTOS.

These great concertos occupy a position of honor in the violin repertory. Aside from their enduring artistic value and the fact that their beauties always find deserved appreciation, from the standpoint of the violinist who plays in public they are artistic Declarations of Independence; they are the eloquent and inspiring documents which supply the proof that Bruch freed himself from all mechanical fetters.

Max Bruch's First Concerto* in G minor, is probably the one most frequently played after Mendelssohn's Concerto, Op. 64. Its popularity is due mainly to its wealth of melodic invention and a freedom of form which at the time it first appeared was novel—the substitution of a melodious Prelude for the customary First Movement of the sonata form—and the fact that it makes no exceptional technical demands upon the performer. This is by no means a reproach; the less so since, in my opinion, no composition meant to be played in public, in the concert hall, may be called "easy."

After five characteristic measures of introduction the solo violin enters with a lovely *Recitativo* commencing on the long sustained G, and slowly ascending in an interrupted scale until the D on the E-string has been reached. A similar *Recitativo* in E flat follows a short intermediate orchestral *tutti;* this time, however, taking on a pronouncedly forceful character from the start, with an energetic *forte*, and gradually subsiding at the *pp* on the long sustained G of the E-string. It is the task of the solo artist to emphasize the difference in mood between these two *Recitatives.* He must demonstrate that the first is supremely dreamy, gentle, half questioning; and that the second, beginning in an energetic manner, gradually dies away in enforced resignation.

---

* Max Bruch, Concerto in G minor, Op. 26. Edited and revised by Leopold Auer, Carl Fischer, Inc., New York.

After the orchestra has repeated the two initial measures and passed on to the *pianissimo*, it develops a very rhythmic figure at letter **A**:

227.

one which serves to prepare the characteristic new theme presented by the solo violin:

228.

continued in the same energetic manner up to three measures before letter **B**, where the lovely phrase:

229.

appears. The composer has provided this one phrase with no less than *three* expression marks, proof positive of the importance he attached to it. It is to be played *broadly*, with *ardent feeling* and with *tone*. Before the *a tempo* an important *ritenuto* should be carefully observed, since it adds to the incisiveness of the *fortissimo* entrance of the orchestra.

After the orchestral *tutti* we have a new cantabile theme for the solo violin:

230.

with a counter-theme in the orchestra. This is one of the loveliest moments in the entire "Prelude" if played with real feeling and tonal warmth. At the *Un poco più lento* the above-mentioned theme repeats an octave higher. The *Tempo primo*, at letter **C**, takes us back again to the characteristic rhythmic figure in the orchestra, as at letter **A**, and to the corresponding

melody in the solo violin part.   This time it appears in the
lower third, in connection with the great working-up *(stringendo*
and *crescendo)* which leads to the climax, the *fortissimo*
entrance of the orchestra, with its brilliant *tutti* and the somewhat modified Recitative of the "Prelude."   This Recitative
concludes with a Cadenza rhythmically divided, for which the
composer has provided the indication Allegro:

I advise the student to *begin this Allegro very quietly* in
order to bring out with major effect a great working-up in tone
and tempo *(stringendo)* in the ascending scale, until the
fortissimo entrance of the orchestra is reached.

The second movement, *Adagio,* is an "Aria," composed of
two principal themes:

and

as well as a secondary theme at letter **D,** which last is first
introduced by the orchestra with a variation in the solo violin:

It should be played with great breadth and a maximum of
tone.   At letter **B** a somewhat more animated tempo is required
in order that the theme with variation at letter **D,** in the

original tempo, already mentioned, may convey an impression of greater breadth. That this is clearly the composer's intention is proven by the fact that he has supplied the indications *pesante*, "with weight," and *non legato* for the variation.

At letter **E** the secondary theme again occurs, this time in the dominant, and it should also be played with a big tone and in a very quiet tempo.

At letter **F** we find what is, perhaps, the loveliest passage in this lovely *Adagio*, the recurring First Theme, this time announced *pianissimo*, in G flat by the orchestra, and repeated by the solo violin *molto espressivo*, "with the utmost expression" and, of course, in a very quiet manner. The variation at letter **G** calls for a somewhat more animated tempo which again takes on breadth at the entrance of the orchestra, two measures before letter **H**, and is played broadly until letters **K** and **L**, after which it grows more and more subdued until it finally dies away:

At the beginning of the Finale of his concerto the composer has written *Allegro energico*, and the player should follow his indication. This *energico* lies in the nature of the theme itself; and the first thing to do to express it is to make a rhythmic accent on the *second half* of *each* of the first two measures:

and to repeat this accent whenever these measures recur. This should be done, however, without in any way forcing the tone, to avoid any distressing scratching during the playing of the chords. These accents are not indicated in the original, yet their observation is of the very greatest importance if the theme is to be properly characterized according to the composer's wish.

Two measures after letter **D** the solo violin again enters, this time on a *fortissimo con fuoco* and in the third and fourth measures following—as at the beginning—we must observe important accents, this time on the second and fourth quarters respectively:

237.

in order to make the desired *con fuoco* practically possible. Somewhat later:

238.

the singing Second Theme is played by the orchestra, and taken over by the solo violin *(fortissimo)* on the G-string, to be spun out in *cantabile* style with incidental interruptions in the orchestra till we reach the graceful variation:

239.

Following the *tranquillo:*

240.

which, played with the wrist alone, should flow lightly over the strings, comes a tonal working-up leading to the Principal Theme in the dominant, *fortissimo*, presented by the orchestra. At letter **G**, as at the beginning, the solo violin presents the Principal Theme, which concludes with a short development. At letter **H** the thematic repetition begins in another key, with an extension to the organ-point on the dominant and a deceptive cadence *(ff,* E flat major) in the orchestra.

From letter **K** on we move rapidly by means of an uninterrupted *stringendo* and a tremendous *Appassionato:*

241.

ff appassionato

to the *Presto con fuoco*. This last, however, should not make
a sudden, precipitate entrance, but should impress the listener
as a natural consequence and culmination of the preceding
stringendo.

In his Concerto No. 2, in D minor,* the composer again
shows a decided preference for a freër and more novel formal
structure. In this work, too, he discards the customary *Allegro*
in order to begin his concerto with an *Adagio, ma non troppo,*
which is not, however, an introduction, but as regards length
and musical content may be considered a principal movement.
In any event it is the most important movement of the entire
concerto, and is followed by a second movement in the guise
of a *Recitative* and *Allegro*, and a third, a *Finale*.

This first movement, the *Adagio*, is a profoundly felt musical
composition which captivates both player and auditor through
an employ of the noblest artistic means of appeal. A rich flow
of melody permeates the entire piece; alternate lyric and
dramatic sections supply a musical picture full of variety; and
there are moments, as well, when passion dominates in the
most violent irruptions of emotion as, for instance, at the entrance of the orchestra with the following violin solo at letter **D**:

242.

At letter **E**, however, this mood is resolved in one of the
gentlest resignation indicated by the *tranquillo:*

243.

p tranquillo

---

* Max Bruch. Concerto in D minor, No. 2. Revised and edited by Leopold
Auer. Carl Fischer, Inc., New York.

and this lovely melody cannot be played too serenely or too intimately in order to mark the contrast between it and the preceding *con passione*. This mood is sustained until the letter **G** is reached, though it is possible, at letter **F**, to make the tempo a trifle more animated and lend the music a steadily growing fulness of tone, especially from the moment on when the composer prescribes a *con molto expressione:*

The whole phrase climaxes on the high C on the E-string:

and I would once more warn the young violinist—as I have already warned him elsewhere—against the danger of forcing his tone in the high positions on the E-string. He is apt to do so at moments such as the one to which we just have alluded, when the music demands the utmost ardency and the player, carried away by emotion, forgets that the tonal power of the violin has its limits. At letter **I**, again, passionate intensity of expression must be developed without, however, increasing the tempo:

The Cadenza which follows should begin and continue with an ever increasing volume of tone and quickening of tempo until toward the end, before the trill:

The trill should be long and sustained in a very pronounced *diminuendo*, while the orchestra presents the first theme, *piano*.

At letter **L** the tempo again grows more animated and agitated until two measures before letter **M**, where the second principal theme (as at letter **E**) returns; this time, however, in the tonic. From letter **O** on the tempo grows gradually slower until the first movement comes to an end.

In connection with the second movement of this concerto, the "Recitative and Allegro," it is very necessary that every violin student should have a clear idea of exactly what "Recitative" means when applied to violin music. The composer supplies the indication: it is the part of the player to express its meaning to the best of his ability; and aside from anything else, this calls for musical instinct, temperament and also a certain amount of experience.

In earlier times, before Wagner, it was possible for aspiring violin students to learn how to phrase a dramatic *recitativo* by listening to the famous opera singers; but in this respect the times have changed. In modern opera the melodies, in most cases, are assigned to the orchestra. There they are covered up or obscured by counterpoint, contrary motion, and imitation on the part of component groups of orchestral instruments, while the singers themselves have to make almost superhuman efforts to pierce these masses of instrumental tone with the human voice. The "Recitative" as it formerly was sung no longer occurs, unless it be a recitative of the *parlando*, the "spoken" type, or occurs as a cry of passion or of horror.

Personally I learned much, in my day, from the famous Italian opera singers who sang at the Imperial Opera in St. Petersburg during the winter months. I also gathered many valuable hints from celebrated German concert singers, artists like Julius Stockhausen, who was a perfected master of the old Italian *bel canto* repertoire. Young violinists of to-day, however, can learn musical recitative declamation only by listening to the great contemporary masters of their own instrument, or to the most important *lieder-singers* of the classic repertoire, for "Recitative," all said and done, is simply declamation expressed in music.

The Bruch "Recitative" in question—in so far as its composer can do so with printed words—has been qualified by indications as clearly as possible, and his music in his connec-

tion with his indications speaks for itself. The initial Recitative, after the orchestral introduction, finds its contrast in the
somewhat agitated *Allegro* which follows it, and which is
interrupted by the orchestra at letter **D**. After two measures
of free recitative by the solo violin the *Allegro* resumes at letter
E, and concludes on the *Andante sostenuto* with the two
measures:

The "Finale," *Allegro molto*, at its beginning should sound
like the rustling of woodland leaves; before long a horn calls
repeatedly in the distance, the call gradually growing louder
until at letter **B** it rings out like a jubilant "hallo." Nearer
and nearer comes the call until the *con brio:*

the passage in sixths storms upward to the high E on the
E-string, and a D major scale leads up in brilliant fashion to
the entrance of the orchestra at letter **C**.

At letter **D**:

a kind of Cadenza is energetically introduced by the solo
violin, a Cadenza whose rhythm, however, is of the strictest.

The various *sforzandi* on the third eighth-note:

give this passage a natural charm. At letter **F** the second motive appears as a contrast to the principal theme:

It is a species of singing *Valse lente*, is presented alternately by the solo violin and the orchestra, and concludes with the graceful variation after letter **H**:

At letter **K** a *much quieter tempo;* a "taking breath" after the orchestra has started the fiery Principal Theme, should be observed. Before the letter **M** we have the great *Allargando:*

which leads us back to *Tempo primo, ff.*

At letter **O** we once more encounter the Second Theme, as at letter **F**. At letter **Q** a long-extended *poco stringendo* commences which leads to a subsequent variation, as after letter **H**; this time, however, in B minor. After letter **S** the tempo is somewhat more animated in order that the charming variation:

(which should be played with a *spiccato bowing*) broadening out tonally to the *sforzando*, may sound quite light and airy. The closing measures before the short chords should be played *détaché*.

CHAPTER XII.

THE BRUCH "SCOTCH FANTASIA."

With genuine musical sensitiveness Bruch chose a sombre tonality—E flat minor—for the sombre Introduction of his "Scotch Fantasia."* It would be difficult to conceive of deep affliction expressed more convincingly in music than in the first eight measures played by the orchestra in this work. Instinctively we think of two masterpieces of the same character: the "Funeral March" in Beethoven's "Eroica" Symphony, and the "Funeral March" in Chopin's Sonata in B flat minor. I conceive Bruch's "Scotch Fantasia" as the death chant of some hero of popular legend, sung by a Scotch bard of old to the accompaniment of the harp. The solo violin begins its *Quasi recitativo* at letter **A**, with the long sustained phrase:

played, of course, on the A-string. It should sound like a sorrowful evocation of an event long since past. This chant or song moves on, without hope and shrouded in endless grief until, from letter **B** to letter **C**, it takes on an increasingly agitated character and at:

culminates in an outbreak of despair which soon, however:

is succeeded by resignation. At letter **C** we again have a wild outcry vibrant with sorrow, which soon dies away, and after

---

* Max Bruch, Scotch Fantasia. Edited and revised by Theodore Spiering. Carl Fischer, Inc., New York.

which the solacing *Adagio cantabile* in E flat major makes
its appearance.

At letter **F** the harp is heard for the first time, supporting
in a majestic manner the beautiful bardic chant. This is the
impression the Introduction always has made on me, one which
I have here attempted to convey to the reader. The violinist
in whom similar impressions are awakened, must strive to shape
up his emotions in his interpretation in order to convince his
listeners. Four measures before letter **I** a still quieter tempo
is absolutely justified, and may be maintained until the
morendo and close is reached. I do not touch upon the technical side of the interpretation since, in my opinion, the
mechanics of both hands, finger and bow-arm must be absolutely
controlled by the player if works such as the Bruch "Scotch
Fantasia" are to be presented in the proper way.

The second movement, the "Dance," begins in a jolly
dance-rhythm. In the seventh measure following letter **A** a
sudden, hesitant *lusinghando:*

is introduced, four measures long, which should be played with
deliberate hesitancy in tempo and with delicate expressiveness.
At letter **B** the merry dance once more recurs with great
energy, keeping on to letter **C**. At letter **D** the composer
insists upon a vigorous *con brio:*

and repeats his demand six measures later. After the orchestral *tutti, fortissimo,* at letter **E**, the graceful theme:

repeats, *piano,* and an octave higher. The whole figure lying
in the high positions on the E string up to letter **G**, should be

played with the utmost delicacy, and with the softest and most mellow quality of tone, especially the chromatic scale:

till the *a tempo* is reached.

At letter **I**:

an exchange of musical thought takes place between the soloist and the flute in the orchestra, until they unite in the passage in thirds and, with a continually increasing volume of tone, are absorbed by the orchestra at letter **K**. Seven measures before letter **L** we have the closing passage. It lies somewhat awkwardly, and yet must sound extremely clear; and with a gradual increase in tempo, moving ever more rapidly, should end with a *molto crescendo*. The *Adagio* after letter **L** has been borrowed from the Introduction, and calls for a beautiful quality of tone, especially at letter **M**:

and though a very long bow-stroke should be used the tone should not be forced.

The third movement, *Andante sostenuto*, is a simple song in folk-tune style, and in keeping with its character must be played with sincere intimacy. From the following passage on:

somewhat greater warmth of expression is demanded.   Three
measures after letter **A**:

266.

p espress.

the folk-tune theme begins in a somewhat more animated tempo
in the orchestra.   At letter **B** a *stringendo* occurs, and the
melody becomes more and more agitated until, in the fourth
measure of the *Più animato*—together with an increasing
working-up in the tone—it assumes a highly passionate character, which mood does not yield to a return of the preceding,
quiet mood until the *Tempo primo* has been reached.   This
quiet mood is of brief duration.   At letter **D** an orchestral
tutti commences which increases in tonal volume until the solo
violin with a most intensive *forte*, and using the long bow sets in:

267.

f

taking over the melody from the orchestra, and continuing it
until letter **E**, where its ardor yields to appeasement.

The "Finale" of the "Fantasia," an *Allegro guerriero*, in
my opinion calls for a qualifying tempo indication: the addition of *ma moderato*.   Its martial motive calls for great energy
in presentation and a moderate tempo.   A moderate tempo
also is indicated by the sixteenth-note figuration in the bass,
at letter **A**.   The last eighth in the first two measures:

268.

ff

should be played as shortly as possible; furthermore the accent
on the last quarter-note:

269.

should be strongly emphasized. This will give the theme its proper character.

The composer wishes the variations which follow to be played *con brio;* the following passage:

270.

spiccato, with a noble tone. At letter **C** we have another mood, *Un poco tranquillo:*

271.

and this passage should be played very expressively; while the succeeding *allargando* should be taken with still greater breadth and according to the composer's indication, with still greater expressiveness. I should prefer to add a *Più allegro* to the *Tempo primo* at letter **D**, since otherwise the variation sounds clumsy; something which the composer certainly did not intend. This variation is meant to supply the contrast to the preceding broad song theme in thirds and sixths, and concludes very gracefully on the chromatic scale:

272.

which must be played tranquilly, and ends *pianissimo* with a *ritenuto* on the two-measure trill on B natural.

At letter **G** a struggle begins between the solo player and the orchestra. The experienced soloist will avoid the battle, and play his chords with sonorous fulness and beauty of tone without any scratchy flavor. In view of the frequent repetition of the Principal Theme at letter **H**, I would advise a "cut"

of five measures, beginning at letter **I**; after this cut has been
observed the soloist may continue at the following point:

Eight measures after letter **K** a further "cut" seems advisable; a cut from the fourth quarter of measure eight:

to the fourth quarter of the tenth measure after letter **L**:

whence the player continues to the end.   At the following
passage:

play very quietly, and allow the solo of the orchestral horn
quartet—one of the loveliest moments in the entire "Fantasia"
—to stand out; while the graceful solo violin passages wind
themselves about the song of the horns, becoming independent
at letter **M**.   Thenceforward, being careful to maintain the
utmost beauty of tone the solo violin plays more and more
slowly up to the following passage:

joining the full orchestra in the *fortissimo* which brings the
work to a close.

CHAPTER XIII.

CAMILLE SAINT-SAËNS.

The late Camille Saint-Saëns' Third Concerto in B minor, Op. 61,* of the three he wrote for the violin, has won the greatest measure of general appreciation. It was first played in public by Pablo de Sarasate, in Paris (January 2, 1881); yet it is no work of merely passing interest, associated with the personality of a single great artist, but one included in the repertories of practically all contemporary solo violinists, men and women.

The First Movement of the Concerto, *Allegro non troppo*, in 2/2 time, begins almost immediately with a theme vibrant with passion in the highest degree and, according to the composer's direction the *non troppo* of the tempo-signature should be carefully observed. This *non troppo* is of the highest importance, for it brings out the heroic-pathetic character innate to the theme, which is enhanced by the accents which occur on nearly every quarter-note, from the beginning until the first orchestral *tutti* is reached. The composer has done all in his power to make his intentions clear, and this passionate mood remains unchanged and uninterrupted in its moderate movement, until the *Tranquillo assai* after letter **B** has been reached. Then we have a four measure preparatory passage, *espressivo*, in a more quiet tempo:

278.

mf espressivo

while at the *Tranquillo assai:*

Tranquillo assai

279.

p

---

* Camille Saint-Saëns, Concerto No. 3, in B minor, Op. 61. Revised and edited by Henry Schradieck Carl Fischer, Inc., New York.

the mood of the music becomes very lyric and passes over into
the beautiful Second Theme in **E** major:

280.

dolce espressivo   *etc.*

which calls for the greatest delicacy and intimate warmth in
rendering in order to establish the lyric character already
mentioned.   This theme is in striking contrast to the Principal
Theme enunciated at the beginning.

At letter **C** the First Theme again appears in a working-out
similar to that at the beginning, and in the same moderate yet
energetic tempo.   At letter **D** the supremely lyric motive, which
first occurs after letter **B**, reappears and should be played
even more quietly than before, if possible; while the maximum
of serenity and delicacy of tone-color should be developed at
letter **E**.   At letters **F** and **G** the First Theme recurs, this
time in the orchestra, the solo violin weaving a series of the
most brilliant passages above it, and thus bringing the first
movement to a close in a very expressive manner.

The *Andantino quasi Allegretto*, the second movement, is
in 6/8 time.   On one occasion, when I met Saint-Saëns in
Paris, the composer told me he was surprised that this second
movement of his concerto, in spite of the above tempo indication—the proper metronome indication would be ♩. =56
which, reduced to eighth-notes, would call for a somewhat
lightly movemented tempo—was nevertheless, often played in
a sentimental and dragging manner, quite contrary to his intention.

Saint-Saëns himself wished this movement to be played
simply and in a quietly flowing manner, without that effect
of passion which lends the two movements in which it is framed
their special character.   It is a melody of the Siciliano type,
which the solo violin sings, and while at letter **B**, the music
sounds as though small clouds were drifting across the blue

Italian skies, this mood does not endure for long. At letter
E all is cheerful again and the charming phrase:

281. *p dolce, tranquillo e semplice*

once more carries us back to the fundamental mood of the
piece. The harmonics at the close must sound very airy, an
effect which may be secured by allowing the bow to pass over
the strings very elastically, without exerting the least pressure:
in addition the composer demands that the music be played
molto tranquillo.

The third movement, *Molto Moderato e Maestoso* in B
minor, 4/4 time, opens with a short Introduction. It is a
species of solo violin recitative with orchestra accompaniment.

In accordance with the composer's indications a very
moderate tempo is appropriate for the Introduction as well as
at the beginning of the *Allegro non troppo;* the former has 4/4
as a time signature, the latter is marked 2/2, *alla breve,* i. e.,
a measure divided into two broad halves. The theme:

282. *f*

should be played with much energy, strictly in time, and with
strong accentuation. At letter A we find a melodious secondary
theme:

283. *p appassionato*

which is full of passionate feeling, especially where the double-
stops occur.

The Introduction and, in particular, the *Allegro non troppo*
which follows it, makes the auditor feel as though an irresistible hurricane were sweeping across the surface of the music
until the *Cantabile* after letter C is reached, where a big

orchestral *tutti* develops, the mood becomes calmer, and the chorale-like Second Theme is taken up, first by the orchestra and a few measures later by the solo violin.

284.

dolcissimo *pp*

At letter **E** the Introduction, and at letter **G** the First Theme recur. The two *staccato* arpeggios, as the player prefer, or in order to facilitate execution, may be played with either an up-bow or a down-bow. The *Più allegro* at the close is a conventional Coda, its style in keeping with that of the composition itself.

Camille Saint-Saëns' "Introduction and Rondo Capriccioso," Op. 28,* for violin and piano, is one of those repertoire pieces which often are subjected to rather brutal treatment, sometimes owing to lack of a correct sense of style on the performer's part, sometimes owing to neglect of the tempo marks and other interpretative indications provided by the composer. Thus it happens that the "Introduction," which Saint-Saëns has marked *Andante malinconico*, is frequently played too rapidly and without the least trace of "melancholy" in expression. The short *Animato*, eight measures long, which the composer wishes played "animatedly" is in most cases— on the concert platform as well as in the studio—sawed off at a galop, in breathless haste. The *Tranquillo* which follows:

285.

ten.

etc.

p

and which leads back to the original tempo at the beginning, is ignored; and as a consequence the short Cadenza is cleared out of the way as speedily as at all possible. The listener does not quite know where he is at until the "Rondo," the *Allegro, ma non troppo*, in 6/8 time is reached, where he again "finds himself" since this has to be played strictly in time.

---

* Camille Saint-Saëns, "Introduction and Rondo Capriccioso." Revised and edited by Gustave Saenger. Carl Fischer, New York.

Its theme is a very graceful one ,and gains an additional
charm when the syncopation is correctly accented:

This syncopation upon which, I might say, the theme itself
is based, recurs on each and every occasion when the theme
itself appears, and forms the musical "backbone" of the entire
composition.   At the theme in C major, in 2/4 time, marked
*Con morbidezza:**

the composer's indication should be exactly observed if the
theme in question is to be given the character desired.   In the
twelfth measure of the section in 2/4 time I advise that the
piano indicated:

be not ignored; for its observance noticeably enriches the tonal
color of the entire measure.   Six measures after letter **E** an
"Intermezzo" appears which has no connection either with
what has preceded or with what follows it. It almost seems as
though the composer had deliberately decided to turn his inspiration into another channel and create something distinctly
novel.   These twenty new measures:

should be played *much more slowly*, and with the most intimate
expression, and are among the loveliest contained in this

* The Italian noun *morbidezza* is one with a wide range of meanings, from
"modesty" to "wantonness."   Musically speaking, *con morbidezza* means "played with
special softness, and excess of feeling tinged with bitterness."

original work. At the twenty-first measure the "Rondo" tempo once more sets in at letter **F**, introduced by a few preparatory measures. The First Theme is reintroduced in the orchestra by means of a few preparatory measures accompanied with self-effacement by the solo violin which then, after some brilliant passage-work, passes to the *Più allegro* at letter **G**. The latter should commence very rapidly, and be played with a very light *spiccato* in order, toward the close, to pass over into a genuine and powerful *détaché* when the *Crescendo molto* ending with the *fortissimo* sets in.

Among the remaining compositions Saint-Saëns has written (aside from his other concertos and the fine chamber-music) is the "Havanaise," Op. 83,* musically one of the most interesting.

The theme of the "Havanaise" seems to be of genuine Spanish origin, and the characteristic triplet with its two succeeding eighth-notes:

290.

is typical, especially with the accent given the last eighth-note in every measure. This peculiarity lends the Theme a Moresco-Spanish, languishing, voluptuous tone which echoes through the entire composition and often recurs in different keys.

After the exposition of the First Theme, *Allegretto lusinghiero,* follows the *Allegro:*

291.

* Camille Saint-Saëns. "Havanaise," Op. 83. Carl Fischer, Inc., New York.

contrasting with the First Theme, and a return to the Tempo I
(Allegretto) is succeeded by a *Molto espressivo:*

The concluding *Allegro, ma non troppo,* with its chromatic
scale in thirds and sixths, as well as the *Più allegro* which
follows it, represent a concession made the virtuoso on the
composer's part.   Six measures before the final *Allegretto*
with the fanfare, which should ring out like a trumpet signal,
the composer once more comes into his own.   This trumpet
signal:

which invites the people who have been merrymaking together
to return home when evening falls, is developed and illustrated
in a masterly manner in the concluding *Allegro:*

and the initial and concluding phrases are the principal musical
moments of this composition which, in its own way, displays
such decided originality of conception.

CHAPTER XIV.

EDOUARD LALO.

For more than fifty years Edouard Lalo's "Symphonie Espagnole,"* Op. 21, has been a favorite repertoire number of one generation after another of young, rising virtuosos, and many retain it even in the maturity of their art. As a "concert piece" the "Symphonie Espagnole" in a single composition offers the violinist a tableau of the development of the technical apparatus of the violin—with the exception of the *staccato*—in the very noblest form and based on purely musical principles. Thanks to its composer's delicacy of perception—he has avoided all the commonplaces into which the lightly flowing wealth of Spanish melody** might have mislead him—it also is one of the most original works of the concert repertoire. Lalo entered into the very soul of this elemental music and in every case revealed only its noblest essence without any external overelaboration. When critics and musical specialists complain of its too frequent appearance on the recital programme, they only emphasize the value of this composition.

The "Symphonie Espagnole" consists of five movements of which *four* (not counting the "Intermezzo," No. 3) at the most cases only *three*—Nos. 1, 4 and 5—are played in public. This last arrangement is to be deplored since the movement elided, the "Scherzando," No. 2, is one of the most original in the work.

In the First Movement, (*Allegro non troppo*) aside from its original theme, the rhythmic combination of one important section is of interest. I refer to the frequent quarter-note triplet:

(Correct phrasing)

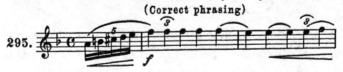

295.

---

* Edouard Lalo. "Symphonie Espagnole," Op. 21. Revised and edited by Gustav Saenger. Carl Fischer, Inc., New York.

** The fact that Lalo's ancestors in the direct line were pure-blooded Spaniards may have something to do with the convincing local color of his work. On the other hand, as Paul Dukas has said: "It is quite as possible that he wrote the 'Symphonie Espagnole' merely because he was the intimate friend of Sarasate, and would have done so even if his forebears had not been Spaniards."

Frequently, and in the studio in particular, the triplet is *hurried*, and thus the theme is robbed of the individual character which gives it its special charm: the triplet should exactly fill out the value of the two quarter-notes which make up the second half of the measure. If this is not done with exactness then the melody when played sounds as follows:

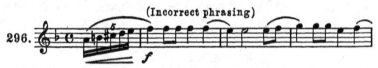

296.

which does the composer an injury, and is contrary to every rule of musical ethics. At the *Dolce espressivo* after letter **D**:

297.

the passage should begin with as soft and delicate a tone as possible, the tone gradually increasing in power until letter **E**, *fortissimo*, is reahed. Two measures after letter **E** the solo violin introduces a counter-theme, *fortissimo*, sounding against the Principal Theme in the orchestra; and while playing it the violin must conform closely to this Principal Theme, and move in strict accord with its rhythm in view of the triplet already mentioned which, as has been said is an essential part of the theme itself. At the following point, midway between letters **I** and **J**:

298.

the composer indicates an *à la corde*, which in French signifies "on the string," the bow being led naturally, with a short *détaché*, and continuing thus until the end of the movement.

With regard to the Second Movement, the real "Scherzando" does not begin until four measures after letter **B**, and the start of the movement rather suggests a tender serenade of the type common to Italy and Spain, the triplet-figuration and the short chords in the accompaniment seemingly conceived for the guitar, and expressive of the national character of the music. At letter **D** the melody turns somewhat more serious, with a pronounced preference for the minor mode. The frequent changes of tempo between the *Tempo primo* and the *Poco più lento* sound like tender questions and ironic replies; and these contrasts of expression in the music should be strongly emphasized and should assume a passionate character from letter **F**:

299.

to letter **G**. At letter H the jocose, *Scherzando* mood again prevails in the music, to be maintained until the two *pizzicati* notes **(G)** at the close.

The Third movement, the "Intermezzo" is not suitable for public performance and hence never is played.

The Fourth Movement, *Andante,* is a lyric song with occasional dramatic moments which lend the entire composition a very serious character. It proves how capable the composer was in making the solo violin express his thoughts, supported by a masterly orchestration. The number, rhythmically, shows an unmistakable Spanish folk-wise character, for all it contains no actual folk-melodies. The Second Theme, at letter **C**:

300.

in particular, demonstrates what has just been said; and the two accents on the third quarter materially aid in producing this impression. The Cadenza together with *Tempo primo* beginning before letter **G** form the climax of this movement.

The Fifth Movement, the "Rondo"—it is marked *Allegro* —is a Finale which, in my opinion, presents the most folkwise themes the whole "Symphonie" contains. The First Theme should be taken very lightly, strictly in time, and with a short *spiccato*. The eighth-rests after each of the two eighthnotes:

if they are clearly emphasized, lend this theme its typically joyous character. It might further be mentioned that the accent on the syncopation falls on the *first* and not on the *second* eighth-note, as for example:

The tempo should not be too rapid a one, so that the passages in sixteenth-notes which follow may sound clear, distinct and unhurried. I would advise playing the octave passage at letter **H** with fingering (fingered octaves) as follows:

After letter **J** take the *Poco più lento* much more slowly. It introduces what might be called the "Toreador Theme"

(one which has nothing in common with that of the "Toreador Song" in "Carmen"):

and which should be *sung* and not *played*, with the most beautiful quality of tone the violinist can produce. The characteristic eighth-rests should be carefully observed; and when the same theme recurs on the A-string, *dolcissimo*, the player must strive to express it with the most intimate and delicate quality of tone he can achieve. At letter **K** we recur to the beginning tempo of the "Rondo," and after letter **Q** beautiful tone-effects may be secured if the trill on the note A:

be played *piano*, and the *pizzicato* A on the same string be taken very sonorously, as though on a harp, with a stiff first finger. The final high D on the E-string, before the two final chords, will sound better if it be played with an up-bow V :

Lalo's "Concerto, Op. 20, and his "Concerto Russe" for violin and orchestra—he also has written a "Fantaisie Norvégienne" and a "Romance-Sérénade"—are both incomparably weaker, musically, than his "Spanish Symphony." Violin virtuosos as famous as Fritz Kreisler and Jacques Thibaud, both of whom belong to the French School, have included neither one nor the other in their concert programmes.

CHAPTER XV.

TSCHAIKOVSKY.

Tschaikovsky's Concerto in D major for violin and orchestra is a work in which its composer unreservedly reveals his individuality, in which he shows a physiognomy which suggests that of none of his predecessors. In "My Long Life in Music" I have dwelt in detail on the reasons why this work is so highly personal and original. Opinions as to its inner values, however, may differ widely. Eduard Hanslick, a critic of the Vienna *Neue Freie Presse* who enjoyed a great reputation in his day—he was an intimate friend and admirer of Brahms and his music, and an anti-Wagnerian—expressed himself very drastically with regard to Tschaikovsky's Concerto when the Russian violinist Adolf Brodsky played it for the first time in Vienna some thirty years ago. Hanslick, whose verdict with regard to the first two movements had been a decidedly cool and negative one, said about the Finale, the third movement, which is entirely folkwise in character, that on hearing it one felt it smelled of vodka,* or to be exact ". . . it suggests savage, vulgar faces, curses, breaths *laden with vodka.*" Quite aside from the questionable taste in suggesting such an olfactory idea in connection with the music of a genuis like Tschaikovsky, there is not the slightest justification for it. I myself have lived many years in Russia and know the people and their customs at first hand. And I have found that the people when they danced and sang on Sundays and festival days danced in the open, in the village street, where the young men and girls moved in graceful rounds to the accompaniment of the mouth-organ and the rhythmic clapping of hands. Where *vodka* is obtainable, in the village inn or tavern, there is no music and no dancing—for the simple reason that the feminine element is missing. Hanslick's remark also is quite illogical: one might just as well claim that Brahms' "Hungarian Dances" smelled of sour country wine, that hearing Johann Strauss' waltzes suggested Vienna lager beer, or that a per-

---

* *Vodka* is the Russian term for the fiery whisky usually distilled from rye, but also from barley and potatoes.

formance of Sarasate's "Spanish Dances" tickled the auditor's palate with the flavor of Madeira.   At any rate, in spite of Hanslick's malicious characterization, the great Russian composer's Concerto in D major has held its own in all the concert halls of the cultured world, and in every studio where rational violin-playing is taught.

In the following interpretative analysis of the Tschaikovsky Concerto the letters refer to my own edition.*   After the orchestral introduction the solo violin enters with a few unaccompanied introductory measures which lead up to the Principal Theme.   The composer's tempo indication is *Moderato assai*, and it is thus that this short introduction should be played: quietly, meditatively and free in expression.   Rhythmically the Concerto begins with the Principal Theme:

At letter **B**

Here the player must keep in strict touch with the orchestra rhythmically ,and later, at the *a tempo*:

very quietly and with a warm quality of tone; yet without broadening out too much, since the music moves serenely in a moderate tempo, and should not become an *Adagio*.   The only change in tempo occurs at the *Poco più mosso*.   Four measures after letter **E** we have a triplet-passage in thirds, ending in thirty-second sextolets which are not found in the original edition of the concerto and which, naturally, are

---

* Peter Tschaikovsky, Concerto in D major, Op. 35.   Revised and edited by Leopold Auer.   Carl Fischer,. Inc., New York.

missing in the orchestra score as well. This passage is one
which I have changed. In order that the solo player may not
lose touch with the orchestra it is most important that he play
the passage in question in the *strictest time and rhythm*. In
the final measure, however, where the chromatic scale in tenths
begins:

310.

a *ritenuto* is permissible, since the orchestra in this measure
holds the same chord.

At letter **F** we come to the variation of the Principal Theme.
It is marked *leggiero*, i. e., to be played with a light *staccato*
bow. At letter **G** we have a little development which leads
over to the brilliant orchestral *tutti* and the bravura Cadenza.
The latter is free in form. It should be played as the performer's own taste and judgment suggests. My pupils play
certain measures with slight changes which I will here indicate:

Instead of:

311.

They play:

312.

and again, instead of:

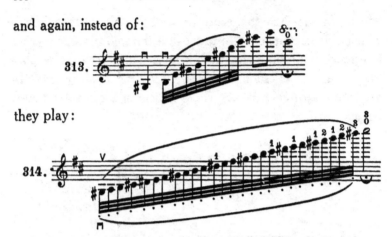

they play:

either *legato* or *staccato*, with V or ⊓ , *ad libitum*.

After the Cadenza the tempo reverts to the *Moderato* first indicated. The *Allegro giusto* after letter **N** should not be taken too rapidly, since in that case the triplets at letter **O**:

become indistinct.

The *Più mosso* which follows, however, may be played in a much quicker tempo and I would advise that it be taken in a 2/2, *Alla breve* rhythm up to the final three measures, which again should be rendered with greater breadth.

"Canzonetta" *(Andante)* is the title of the second movement. I would substitute "Canzone" for it. Its music does not sound like a "songlet" but like a beautiful, serious "song." At letter **B** (from this point on I advise the student to drop his mute and play *senza sordino)* the music grows more exalted, wellnigh passionate. The tone should sound forth free and unhampered up to the return of the first Theme, after letter **C**. Unfortunately it is impossible to affix the *sordino* to the instrument again, hence the player must try to produce a soft, dampened tone, thus artificially securing a *sordino* effect.

The third movement is an *Allegro vivacissimo*. The composer wished this movement to be played as "quickly and animatedly as possible." I have—*with Tschaikovsky's consent and approval*—deleted a few repetitions. These cuts are exactly indicated. If the soloist is to play it with orchestra accompaniment he should have his own orchestra parts and an orchestra score, in which the cuts have been exactly entered, or else he should play in accordance with the original, making no cuts. After the orchestral prelude the solo violin begins alone; and the student should play with freedom, as though playing a cadenza until the *Tempo primo* is reached. Then, however, he must play strictly in time; emphasizing the ━━━ meticulously and using a light *spiccato bowing*.

At letter **C** we have a short "breathing spell" in a somewhat quieter tempo *poco meno mosso,* yet before long the *Tempo primo:*

316.

returns, and the music again reverts to a merry mood and continues with a working-up in tone till we reach the *Molto meno mosso.* Here the tempo is much slower and at the *espressivo:*

317.

the student should play very singingly up to the *Tempo primo* which follows, and which has been prepared by a *sempre stringendo.* From this point on the Finale offers no new developments until its close.

In addition to his concerto, Tschaikovsky wrote some shorter compositions for violin and piano, and the graceful "Sérénade mélanconique" (dedicated to me) and which—also with orchestral accompaniment—appeared before the Violin Concerto. There is also a "Mélodie,"* which I have revised and a "Scherzo"** edited by Zimbalist.

---

* P. Tschaikovsky, "Melodie." Revised and edited by Leopold Auer. Carl Fischer, Inc., New York.

** P. Tschaikovsky, "Scherzo." Revised and edited by Efrem Zimbalist. G. Schirmer, New York.

My knowledge of Tschaikovsky transcriptions for violin and piano practically is confined to those which I myself have made. Aside from the "Mélodie" already mentioned, they include: the "Andante Cantabile" from the String Quartet in D major; a "Valse" from the Suite for String Orchestra; and the "Air de Lensky," from Tschaikovsky's opera "Eugen Oneguine." Mischa Elman has made a highly effective transcription of the song: "Ye Who Have Yearned Alone." With the exception of the Elman transcription, which is issued by Schirmer, the others are published by Carl Fischer, Inc. All these transcriptions are intended for the concert stage, and often appear on the recital program. There are other transcriptions as well, notably those by Arthur Hartman; but I am unaccquainted with them.

Chapter XVI.

GLAZOUNOW, RIMSKY-KORSAKOFF AND DVOŘÁK.

The Concerto for violin in A major, Op. 82, by Alexander Glazounow* is one which I myself have seen take shape. It is dedicated to me and it was played by me for the first time in public in Petrograd, in February, 1906, the composer conducting, at a concert of the Imperial Russian Musical Society.

It consists of three movements interconnected without a stop. It is predominantly lyric in character, allowing the violin to "put its best foot foremost," and is one of the best violin concertos written since the beginning of the twentieth century.

The concerto commences with a very songful theme on the G-string, and this song theme, in the most varied forms, is only occasionally interrupted and then only in a logical manner until the Cadenza—which appears in my edition without change, as the composer set it down in his original Mss.—has been reached.

At No. 20:

318.

---

* Alexander Glazounow, Concerto in A major, Op. 82. Revised and edited by Leopold Auer. Carl Fischer, Inc., New York.

the tempo should grow somewhat more animated and the two
staccato sixteenth-notes should be played very lightly, from the
wrist.   At No. 22 the tempo should become decidedly slower;
at No. 23, the movement is again more passionate and animated
until No. 25 has been reached, where an *Animato* has been
indicated by the composer which holds good until No. 26,
where it is suspended by a *tranquillo.*

The Cadenza, musically as well as technically, represents
the weightiest moment of the entire concerto.   First of all,
each of its themes must be *clearly enunciated*, in spite of all
the figurations and chromatic embroideries in the lower voice.
The difficulty lies in presenting the Principal Theme with *more
tone* while the accompanying figures are produced with *less
tone.*   And this *must* be done if the composer's meaning is to
be expressed and its audition made easily comprehensible to
the auditor.

I would start by advising that the Cadenza be taken in a
very broad tempo, *Moderato assai.*   At the *Più sostenuto:*

play with even greater breadth up to the climax:

Later we have the *Animando* in 2/4 time, which moves in
a livelier measure up to the entrance of the *Allegro* in 6/8 time
which forms the last movement.   For this theme the composer
demands a *Marcato:*

This we may obtain by playing the first two notes of every
measure with a firm *staccato* and with a sharp accent in the
second and third measures. The student must see to it, of
course, that he avoids producing a scratchy quality of tone in
this connection. At No. 36, *Grazioso*, play somewhat more
quietly; and at No. 38, where a singing secondary theme:

appears, hold back a trifle in the tempo and produce the little
swells by means of a light left-hand *vibrato* rather than
a special bow *crescendo*. At No. 40 we revert to the first
tempo with the merry expression of the new theme on the
G-string which in the orchestra leads to a short Canon. Four
measures before No. 49 we find indicated a *Sempre animando*
and at No. 49 a *Più animato* whose observance I advise
because this moment marks the continuous development of an
increasingly rapid tempo, which at Nos. 60 and 61 has become
a *Presto*, and at Nos. 63 and 64 nearly reaches *Prestissimo*.

A rather unique Russian work is Nicolai Rimsky-Korsakoff's
"Fantaisie de Concert sur des thèmes Russes" (Concert Fantasy on Russian Themes"), Op. 33.* Aside from the musical
value of this Fantasy, it has a certain historical interest in so
much as it is the sole work the composer of "Le Coq d'Or,"
"Sniegourotschka" ("The Snow Maiden"), "May Night,"
the symphonic poem "Schéhérazade," etc., has written for
the violin.

The work is based on Russian folk-songs but little known
outside the borders of their homeland. And the fact that the
interest of novelty is added to that of charm and interest of
theme should suffice to recommend the "Fantasy" to the attention of virtuosos playing in concert, for it will help them infuse
new blood into the antiquated recital repertoire, which continually repeats the same numbers. In my revision I have
somewhat shortened the work and made a few slight changes

* Nicolai Rimsky-Korsakoff. *Fantasie de Concert sur des Thèmes Russes,* Op. 33.
Revised and edited by Leopold Auer, Carl Fischer, Inc., New York.

and in its present form it lies within the technical reach of
every routined violinist.

The Cadenza at the beginning of the "Fantasy" I have not
touched. It is admirable as it stands, and the reviser of a work
should never forget that any amendment of an original must
have an absolute ethical or practical justification. If he bears
this fact in mind he will avoid "taking liberties" and his amend-
ments will be constructive and of positive value.

The *Lento* at letter **B**:

should be played with great breadth; and the arpeggio passage
after letter **C**:

should be taken *saltando*, the bow being dropped lightly on
the strings in such a way that each individual one of the eight
notes is clearly and plainly audible.

At letter **E** the student should bear in mind that the *Allegretto grazioso* must really be played "gracefully," and that
in order to do so he must not play too rapidly at the beginning.
A little later we have a *Più vivo*, played with a *saltando* bow:

something which is not easy to do, for only a loose wrist-action
and a loose bow will enable the player to execute this bowing
in a perfected manner. The passage in question, in the original

edition of the "Fantasy," is marked with an alternate *pizzicato* and *arco*, as follows:

This is an imitation of the *balalaika*, the three-stringed guitar popular among the Russian peasantry.

At letter **G**—the *Meno mosso*—play quietly and singingly up to the *Allegro vivace*, letter **H**, where:

the music suddenly grows brisk and merry, a complete change of mood.

After letter **I** we have the Cadenza, *ad libitum*, and at letter **K**, the *Andante tranquillo*, the First Theme is introduced in the orchestra to a tremolo accompaniment by the left hand in the solo violin. At letter **L** the same motive:

is taken up by the solo instrument and leads over at letter **M** to the *Allegro vivace* and close.

Among Slavic composers, the Bohemian Dvořák, who himself played both violin and viola, has furnished the literature of the former instrument with a notable work in his Concerto in A minor, Op. 53, for violin and orchestra.* It possesses that genuine Czech folk-color, that contrast of alternate moods of melancholy and naive happiness which is characteristic of most of Dvořák's compositions, no matter what their form may be, and its spontaneity and wealth of invention justify Brahms' jesting remark that it turned him green with envy to see the things Dvořák thought of off-hand.

---

* To my knowledge it exists only in the original edition published by Simrock, Berlin.

In the First Movement the solo violin, after a short orchestral introduction, enters with a sorrow-laden theme in thirds.
Here the composer has indicated an *Allegro non troppo;* yet
if the serious depth and beauty of the theme are to be revealed
adequately, I would suggest substituting the direction: *Moderato assai.*

At letter **A** the orchestra comes into its own and exposes the
thematic contents of the First Movement which, owing to their
Slavic origin are for the most part in minor keys.   Five
measures after letter D we have the songful theme in C major:

329.

which is soon followed by a short, graceful *Scherzando.*

At letter **E** the development begins in the orchestra with the
First Theme as a basis, and there is a somewhat dry passage
in the solo violin which soon takes on the character of a study
in various bowings.   In my opinion, and nothwithstanding the
notable importance of the First as well as the Second Themes
from the standpoint of invention, the obtrusion of such uninteresting technical episodes make the success of a work problem-
atical.   This may be in a measure responsible for the fact that
though a fine and noble imaginative quality is outstanding in
the Second as well as in the Third Movement of the Dvořák
Concerto, and the instrumentation of the orchestral score is
masterly, this composition is seldom heard on the concert stage.

The *Adagio non troppo* which forms the Second Movement
presents a *cantabile* theme which little by little gains in breadth
until, at letter **I**, it introduces one of the loveliest episodes in
the entire concerto:

330.

At letters **K** and **L**, *Più mosso,* we have a very energetic
motive in contrast to the first, lyric one, and at the *Un Poco
tranquillo, quasi Tempo primo,* before letter **M**, the Second
Theme appears in the orchestra to a graceful variation by the

solo violin. At letter **P** the lovely phrase introduced at letter **J** returns and quietly leads over to the close in a mood of serene quietude.

The Third Movement (Finale), is an *Allegro giocoso, ma non troppo.* It begins with a really jolly theme, and the joyous accent which falls on the first quarter of each second measure:

lend the theme its glowing vitality and character. Eight measures after letter **C** we have a secondary theme in the orchestra, with a pungent *spiccato* passage for the solo violin:

as a variation of the theme itself. After letter **F** comes the Second Theme, which might be entitled *Valse lente,* and which in keeping with the suggestion should be played quietly and expressively:

In connection with it we have a figure which is not easy, rhythmically speaking:

especially since in the orchestra the accent falls on the third eighth.

At letter **K** we have a beautiful Slavic folk-theme with that fundamental melancholy of mood common to the majority of Slavic melodies. Then, after the First Theme and the *Valse lente* theme have once more appeared, the latter in the tonic, the Coda brings the movement to a close in the uusal way.

CHAPTER XVII.

THE ELGAR VIOLIN CONCERTO.

The Violin Concerto Op. 61, in B minor, by Edward
Elgar, in my opinion is next to Tschaikovsky's, the most
important written during the last two decades. For although
it may not possess the depth of Brahms' music nor the sheer
individuality of theme shown in Tschaikovsky's work, it is a
composition of high distinction as regards invention, form and
collective development, the work of a master. This being the
case it seems natural to ask why the work so seldom is found
on the symphony concert programme either in Europe or
America? Is it because of the difficulties of the orchestral
score or the solo part, or is it because the expenditure of time
needed for rehearsals seems too great?

I have only heard this Concerto played in public twice and
then by two virtuosos of the first rank: Fritz Kreisler, who
performed it in London and Jascha Heifetz, here in New
York. In both instances the work scored a great success, one
even greater perhaps, than that obtained by the Brahms' Concerto when it first appeared as a novelty on the concert programmes, introduced to the public by a master of Joachim's
calibre, in spite of violent attacks by part of the press. It may
be that the exceptional length and the weaker third movement
of the Elgar work have militated against its popularity.

In any event it presents great technical as well as musical
difficulties, both for the interpreting solo artist and the orchestra
conductor because of its uninterrupted changes of tempo, often
occurring at intervals of three or four measures, or even less.
There is also the highly interesting polyphonic development
especially in the first and third movements. Its counterpoint
and contrapuntal subjects in the orchestra often crush the solo
violin, with the result that the untrained ear cannot clearly
grasp the melodic development and is dissatisfied. As regards
the constant tempo alternation we feel that the composer has
striven to express his wishes on paper as clearly as possible.
Whether he has succeeded in so doing the future alone can tell.

In the First Movement *(Allegro)* after the orchestra has announced the Principal Themes, the solo violin presents the introductory theme on the dominant in a somewhat hesitant, fragmentary manner; and four measures after No. 10, the First Theme:

is introduced. It is succeeded (No. 16) by a highly lyric Second Theme:

which including its second section (No. 17), may be regarded as one of the loveliest episodes the First Movement contains. At No. 20 the music grows more animated; and two measures after No. 21, a brilliant passage:

gradually leads up to the great *tutti* at No. 23. Four measures after No. 27 the Second Theme makes its entrance in the orchestra against a contrary movement in triplets:

in the solo violin part, *più lento*. No sooner has this movement begun, however, than it changes in the next measure to an *animato* and during the measures which immediately follow continues to alternate between *a tempo, animato* and *largamente* up to No. 29, where a *Lento* is indicated. Five measures

before No. 35 we find a most dramatic variant of the Second
Theme:

which reaches the climax of its subsequent development at No.
41. From this point on the music becomes more and more
agitated, increasingly *animato* (No. 42) and not long after
con fuoco, thence hurrying irresistably on to the end of the
First Movement.

In the Second Movement, the *Andante*, with its beautiful
themes, is contained the vital pith and marrow of the entire
concerto, one which may be destined to survive many another
recent concerto despite the weakness of the last movement.

This *Andante* commences in the solo violin part with a
Counter Theme (No. 45); and its Principal Theme is not
introduced until two measures before No. 46, and only four
measures later the solo violin resigns it to the orchestra. These
two themes appear in constant alternation in the orchestra and
solo parts on a parity of musical importance and together form
a unified whole.

At No. 47 we have a beautiful orchestral episode which
returns (No. 53) and gains an enhanced charm from the
variant developed by the solo violin. At No. 57 the two
themes appear simultaneously, as in the beginning, and in conclusion the composer once more passes in review all the phrases
contained in this *Andante* so rich in melodies.

The Third Movement, *Allegro Molto*, opens with a very
animated introduction. Its quintuplets crowd almost joyously
upward in their ascending flight, and are followed by scales
in octaves and chromatic harmonics:

One expects more than the composer offers in his Principal Theme (No. 68). At No. 73 the Second Theme:

is introduced, and after ten measures passes over into the orchestra in a varied form. The composer calls for a *Più lento*, which is well motived in view of the complexity of the variation.

At No. 94 we encounter a beautiful motive from the Second Movement *(Andante)* this time presented as an *allegro:*

yet grateful after all the preceding passage-work.

The Cadenza (No. 101) forms one of the Concerto's most interesting episodes. It is based on two themes from the First Movement, and provided with an incidental orchestral accompaniment which supports the solo violin in a highly artistic and unobtrusive manner.

This idea is not a novel one. In Joachim's "Concerto in the Hungarian Style" which was published over fifty years ago, an incidental orchestral accompaniment is employed in the Cadenza of the initial movement. Whether Joachim was the first to avail himself of this new effect I cannot say positively. In Elgar's case the Cadenza has been shaped by a master hand; and the fact that the harp is the outstanding instrumental support of the solo violin gives the Cadenza an especially rhapsodic quality. And it should be interpreted in that sense, with freedom, independence and even a hint of the fantastic. After the Cadenza the movement swiftly hastens to a colorful close by means of various changes of tempo.

Chapter XVIII.
CÉSAR FRANCK AND CHAUSSON.

César Franck (1822-1890) has composed a Sonata in A major* for violin and piano which, written in 1886, and dedicated to Eugène Ysaye, universally known and justly famous, is one of the most played chamber music compositions of the present day. Like Beethoven's "Kreutzer Sonata," it is a chamber music composition which has become naturalized on the concert stage. Its popularity dates from the time Ysaye carried it triumphantly through all civilized lands and their concert halls, and it is still a favorite with the present generation of violinists.

The First Movement abandons the usual introductory *Allegro* in favor of an *Allegretto ben moderato* or, rather a *ben moderato* without the "Allegretto." The violin must "breathe out" the questioning initial phrase, which has been compared to "a glance cast toward the infinite," and should be supported in similar fashion by the pianoforte *pianissimo*.

343.

The melody should produce the impression of a song coming from distant, celestial spheres. Five measures after No. 1 there is a slight swell in tone:

344.

which appears only to vanish . At Nos. 2 and 3 we have the great crescendo with its powerful, insistent *ritenuto*, played *fortissimo*:

345.

---

* César Franck, Sonata in A major, for violin and piano. Carl Fischer, Inc., New York.

and from this point on until No. 5 is reached the piano
dominates. At No. 7 the violin reintroduces the initial theme.
The mood of the entire movement remains unchanged up to
a final exclamation:

346.

three measures before the end.

The Sonata as a whole has been very truly and beautifully
summed up as the expression of a soul which offers its sorrows
and renunciations to God. In the First Movement the player
must supply out of his own soul the proper "exteriorization"
of its tears and grief.

In the Second Movement *(Allegro)*, the piano first introduces the passionate theme which is repeated at No. 1 by the
violin. At No. 6 the mood grows quieter; and the *Quasi
Lento* at No. 8 calls for a sorrowfully expressive rendering.
At the Tempo primo:

347.

from No .9 to No. 11, we have the climax of this movement,
outstanding in every way. At letter 19, the Coda commences:

348.

and rushes with hurricane fury to the end. In this movement
human love is carried into the regions of vision, and in its conclusion human yearning strives upward toward the ideal with
elemental passion and intensity.

The Third Movement, with the indication *Ben moderato,*
is a "Recitative-Fantaisie." This is the most difficult of all
the four movements to interpret. The composer, however, has
indicated his own wishes with the most painstaking exactness

and scrupulous care.   Every line of his music is provided with
one or more expression marks, indications for change of tempo,
and dynamic signs, a proof of the major importance he attached to the correct interpretation of this particular movement.   It might be called a supreme prayer of sorrow, one
phrased with the utmost intensity of expression, and one which
the player must *feel* in order to convey to his listeners.

The violin is the leading voice, while the piano part adapts
itself closely to it and supports the solo instrument in its various
shadings of expression.   After No. 4 the bowing in the quiet,
flowing sixteenth-note passage may be altered by the player to
suit his individual needs: though if he intends to do so, the
most absolute calm, equality of tempo and an imperceptible
change of bow are the first requisites.

From No. 10 on:

349.

the greatest energy must be exerted, while beginning with No.
11 the movement progresses in a *Molto lento* to its close.

The concluding Fourth Movement (*Allegretto poco mosso*),
is written almost altogether in the form of a canon.   It offers
a contrast of serenity which the auditor appreciates after the
"Recitative-Fantaisie," and is an expression of the infinite
recognition of the mortal who has risen victorious in his struggle
for mastery of self, and whose soul turns whole-heartedly to
the Divine.   It might be said to breathe the serenity of the
soul which has overcome the earthly and has entered into
perfect beatitude.

At Nos. 11 and 13 we have a reminiscence of the preceding movement and at No. 19 a *Poco animato* leads us to the
close of this interesting work.

A concluding movement in canon form in César Franck's
case has no element of surprise.   As regards form, all the
movements of the Sonata in A minor—unless we except the
first, which probably is musically the most genuinely inspired—
show that counterpoint was its composer's native tongue, and

that in composition he enjoyed the technical facility the organist shows in thematic modulation and improvisation.

From the standpoint of interpretation the difficulties of the composition are obvious. The whole work may be regarded as four evolutions of the human soul toward the Divine. Its sorrow is mystic: in playing the sonata the violinist has to express at times a feeling of anguish withheld, of tears which cannot flow. And the serene joy of the last movement is not of this earth. Most violinists are too apt to express an earthly and human rather than a celestial and spiritual happiness in their playing of the *Allegretto meno mosso*, but the violinist who wishes to do justice to the Sonata in A major in his interpretation must approach it with a reverence, like the officiant at some sacred mystery.

It was a pupil of César Franck, Ernest Chausson (1855-1899), who in his "Poème" for violin and orchestra, Op. 25,* added to serious violin literature an especially noble work which holds its own on the concert stage. It would be difficult to select for this composition, which Richard Wagner inspired, a more appropriate title than the one it bears. The musical repertoire contains a sufficiency of Reveries, Legends, Nocturnes, Ballads and what not, yet none of these terms would have done justice to the rich imaginative content of Chausson's composition.

The long sustained B flat with which the violin sets in after the well-found, mysterious orchestral introduction, must be played with the most beautiful quality of tone the student can produce, and this applies as well to the succeeding Principal Theme (unaccompanied), which must be presented very quietly, and in a most sustained manner. The composer expressly supplies the character indication in the phrase *Lento e misterioso*.

Although Chausson has indicated the bowings with fairly happy results, every player is at liberty to change one or another should it not suit him, and the change can easily be carried out because the tempo is so slow. At the same time the melodic flow and continuity must not suffer, and change of

---

* Ernest Chausson, "Poème," for violin and piano. Breitkopf & Härtel.

bow must take place *inaudibly*, a point which, when the change
is carried out at so difficult a place as that at No. 4, in which
two voices appear, is of the utmost importance.

A few measures before No. 5 a spirit of restlessness develops
and at the subsequent *Animato:*

the mood of the music for a moment becomes highly exalted;
quieting down again, however, at No. 7. Two measures before No. 1:

the student should commence quietly, and drive forward with
ever increasing speed to No. 10, the *Molto animato.* At No.
11, *A tempo animato* he must play very delicately and airly—
the Italian term *flottato* which the composer uses, literally
means "as though floating"—but the music develops a great
tonal *stretto* to the *fortissimo* at No. 12.

At Nos. 14 and 15 we have the recapitulation of the First
Theme which beginning at No. 17:

gradually becomes more and more agitated. From No. 18
on this agitation increases to actual breathlessness, until No.
20 is reached, where the theme enters vigorously in the bass,
and continues fortissimo in the orchestra until it climaxes at
No. 21. The mood now grows quieter and the "Poème"
finally dies away in the trills of the descending quarter-notes.

CHAPTER XIX.

BAZZINI, SARASATE, HUBAY.

My intention in this volume has been to confine my considerations anent interpretation to my own ideas of how the outstanding master-works of violin literature should be played. I have tried to select for interpretative analysis such works as are preëminent and with which every advanced student, sooner or later, *must* become acquainted if he is to lay claim to any real knowledge of the noblest creative achievements in the literature of his chosen instrument.

These great individual violin works may be said to rank with those of Shakespeare, Dante, Goethe, Balzac, Tolstoi, in general literature; with those of Phidias and Rodin in sculpture; Michelangelo, Raphael, Rembrandt, Titian, in painting. The scope of my book does not admit of consideration of hundreds of compositions by distinctive creative and interpreting artists which are to be found on recital programmes of the present day.   Yet I have selected *three* different composers and a work by each to represent *two* different types of composition, one important educationally, the other a type-form in evidence in nearly every recital programme.

The first type of composition is the recital number which is *not* played in public, but which has certain educational and technical merits that give it a definite value. Antonio Bazzini (1818-1897), has written a "Ronde des Lutins" which to this day finds a place on the programmes of the younger virtuosos.   It is an effective show piece, like so many others of its ilk, but the same composer's "Allegro di Concert"* is a far better illustration of the kind of composition which is educationally useful though seldom or never heard in public.

Bazzini's "Allegro di Concert" dates from the middle of the nineteenth century, and shows the influence the Paganini Concertos exerted on its composer when he was a young, ambitious virtuoso eager to make a name for himself on the concert stage.   Bazzini did not develop into a mere virtuoso violinist,

---

* Antonio Bazzini. Allegro di Concert. Revised and edited by Leopold Auer. G. Schirmer, Inc., New York.

for as he matured he became an earnest student and admirable interpreter of Bach and Beethoven. His "Allegro di Concert," however, reveals the virtuoso influence. Why the composer chose to write it in a single movement has never been quite clear to me. Was it a craving to display his originality which led him to ignore the three-movement form of the concerto and end his "Allegro" with a *pianissimo?* If so, it showed considerable daring on the composer's part to venture on an innovation which seemed quite unmotived seventy-five years ago.

During my entire career as a solo artist and a teacher I do not recall ever having heard the "Allegro di Concerto" played in public. Ordinarily this would not speak highly for its musical value, and yet the composition is melodious in a spontaneous Italian way and is not without a certain harmonic richness. It is as technical material, however, that it is really valuable, and when properly used is especially useful in left hand development. Quite aside from any musical value it may possess it offers an ideal preparatory study for the two concertos in F sharp minor, by Ernst and Wieniawski, respectively, and as such I have often used it for those of my pupils who were far advanced.

The "Allegro di Concert" begins in the same key — D major—as Paganini's Concerto No. 1. At letter **G** we encounter a very tuneful Second Theme:

and at letter **H** the traditionally written passage which follows:

one which, however, should be played *piano* the first time and *forte*, with a *détaché*, when repeated.

After the great orchestral *tutti*, we find at letter **N** a new theme, presented in chords:

355.

f risoluto

which should be played with great breadth, and which leads over into the Second Theme already mentioned, the latter now appearing a third higher, in F major.

After letter **R** the Initial Theme recurs with some minor variants and is followed by the passage in thirds as at letter **H**, the passage this time appearing in the tonic, in D major. And then we reach the most interesting portion of the entire work, the Closing Cadence. To play it properly the student must use a very light wrist-action for the *saltato* arpeggios across the strings, and strong, fully developed fingers of more than normal length are essential if some of the stretches toward the end of Cadenza are to be carried out. Then—as already has been mentioned—this "Allegro di Concert" terminates in a *pianissimo, morendo*.

The second type of composition, one which is a feature of practically all contemporary recital programmes, is one which represents the development of characteristic folk-tune melodies in brilliant and idomatic recital numbers. The folk airs and dance tunes of practically every nation have been drawn upon to supply pieces of this description and in some instances—as in Fritz Kreisler's developments of distinctively Viennese airs—they even reflect the musical folk-wise character of a particular city. A native of Hungary, I have preferred to discuss two distinctively Hungarian compositions of this type, both pieces often heard in the concert hall.

Pablo de Sarasate, for whom Lalo wrote his "Symphonie Espagnole" and Bruch his "Schottische Fantasie," is a composer often preferred for the closing number of a recital programme. His numerous books of "Spanish Dances" when they first began to appear, and the composer played them in his own inimitable manner, roused the greatest excitement in the violin world and stirred up concert audiences in general . And

Sarasate's "Fantasie sur Thèmes de l'Opéra 'Carmen,'" his "Zapateado," his "Introduction et Tarantelle" and his "Zigeunerweisen"* ("Gypsy Airs"), Op. 20, are to be found on the recital programmes of the most famous violin virtuosos to-day.

Sarasate, a *Spaniard* by birth, was destined to compose what, perhaps, deserves to be called the most brilliant piece on *Hungarian* airs ever written. A born Hungarian and the composer of a "Hungarian Rhapsody,"** I am the first to admit it, for Sarasate's composition fully justifies its title. It is written absolutely in the style and character of that original type of music which one may hear played at its best in the large *cafés* and restaurants of Budapest, the Hungarian capital.

A Gipsy Hungarian orchestra seldom consists of more than eight or at the most twelve members, and includes a zimbalon-player who manipulates the national instrument with more or less virtuosity. The zimbalon is so well-established in Hungary and Roumania that a Gipsy orchestra without a zimbalon is something quite inconceivable. And the music of these little ensembles—which sometimes include players of great talent—has inspired the compositions in the Hungarian style written by Franz Liszt, Hector Berlioz, Johannes Brahms and Pablo de Sarasate.

It is not generally known, perhaps, that all melodies and dances (*čzardas*) played by the Gipsies are based on folk-songs the first word of whose opening line supplies the title by which they are known among the people. Every "lead" violinist and zimbalon-player embroiders the air of his song with his own original arabesques, ornaments and cadenzas as he sees fit, without in the least degree interrupting the flow or continuity of the ensemble playing. And it is this independence of interpretation, this improvisational quality, which lends the Gipsy music its peculiar charm.

Sarasate, in his "Gipsy Airs" adheres absolutely to the style of the *tzigane* originals as he had heard them played; no son

---

* Pablo de Sarasate. "Zigeunerweisen" ("Gipsy Airs"). Revised and edited by Gustav Saenger. Carl Fischer, Inc., New York.

** Leopold Auer. "Hungarian Rhapsody." Kistner, Leipsic.

of the Hungarian soil could have improved upon him.   In
the Introduction the melancholy mood dominates; the melody
is presented by the violin together with the wellnigh uninterrupted cadenzas which imitate those of the zimbalon, thus
reflecting the distinctly racial character of the music.   The following air, played with the mute:

which precedes the *Allegro* is one of the loveliest, and when
properly interpreted makes a profound impression on the
listener.

The "Allegro molto vivace":

supplies a most characteristic contrast: first we have tears,
tears of undying sorrow and then, immediately after, a transport
of wildest joy, a contrast peculiar to all Hungarian folk-music.

With regard to the tempo the impeccable execution of the
following passage:

will supply the norm of rapidity in which the movement should
be played; immediately after it the tempo increases in swiftness
until the close of the composition is reached.

Without exception all that Sarasate has written calls for a
perfected bow and finger technique, good taste and elegance
in phrasing, and keen sensibility for proper tone-color and
tempo on the part of the player if the effects which lie hidden
in the music are to be adequately exploited.

Jenö Hubay (b. 1858), a master violinist and one of the
most notable virtuoso of his day, soon gave up the concert
platform to divide his time between composition and teaching
at the Academy of Tonal Art in Budapest of which Franz
Liszt in his time was the honorary president. Aside from
various operas and four violin concertos, he has written a
number of brilliant pieces for violin and piano, among them
a "Carmen Fantasy," a "Ballade," "Valse," "Zephyr" and
others which are favorite numbers of the recital repertoire.
Probably the most popular of all is his "Hejre Kati,"*
(Scènes de la Czarda,"** No. 4) which may be considered a
pendant to Sarasate's "Zigeunerweisen."

The music shows at once that the composer has drawn from
the folk-wise font, for its three little movements—*Lento, ma
non troppo, Allegro moderato,* and *Presto*—are all built up
on folk-airs and are so interconnected as to form a complete
whole.

The *Lento, ma non troppo* supplies a tuneful Introduction
for the *Allegro moderato:*

359.

which, in view of the *Presto* succeeding it should be played
decidedly *moderato* in order to mark the contrast between the
tempos. The Introduction will gain materially in effect if it
be taken somewhat in *Tempo rubato*, yet not forgetting that
this *rubato* treatment of the air as regards tempo, must be based
on the *Lento* prescribed.

The *Presto* is a racy, full-blooded Hungarian "Czardas,"
in which the E minor section:

360.

supplies a welcome contrast to the one in E major which recurs
with renewed vigor and brilliancy before the close.

---

* Jenö Hubay. "Hejre Kati." Scénes de la Czarda, No. 4. Carl Fischer,
Inc., New York.

** *"Czarda"* in English means "Inn," a tavern situated on a highroad in the
country.

CHAPTER XX.

TRANSCRIPTIONS, AND MUSICAL MEMORY.

With regard to transcriptions—which to-day form an integral portion of the violinistic concert repertoire—a list of several hundred titles would only in part cover the many compositions either directly transcribed, or paraphrased and re-adapted from the original works of older and newer masters.

The artistic validity of the transcription has been largely discussed. Some deprecate transcriptions altogether; others regard them with condescending tolerance, treating them as though their transfer from another source had branded them with a musical bar sinister. Still others welcome any and all transcriptions with enthusiasm. To my thinking it is not a question of a principle being motived. To me every transcription represents an individual accomplishment, to be judged purely on its own individual merits. If the transcription of a musical idea originally conceived for the voice or some other instrument takes shape as a musically worthy, interesting and idiomatic violin piece—then that is what it is. Any further discussion anent it seems as negligible as, let us say in the case of a good American citizen, whether he were native or foreign born. And of late years, in particular, the musical standing and quality of both transcribers and their transcriptions has practically established the violin transcription as a feature of the recital programme and greatly enriched its repertoire.

Fritz Kreisler unquestionably stands at the head of those whose achievement in the field of violin transcription and paraphrase has been most notable. His transcriptions of older Italian masters of the eighteenth century constitute a definite enrichment of the violin repertoire, and this applies as well to his fine original compositions such as his "Liebesleid," "Liebesfreud," "Caprice Viennoise" and others.

Then we have the masterly transcriptions of Brahms' "Hungarian Dances" by Joseph Joachim; the three Chopin "Nocturnes" respectively transcribed, the one in E flat by Pablo de Sarasate; the one in D major by August Wilhelmj;

and the one in E minor by myself. I will pass from mention of my own Beethoven and Schumann transcriptions to a number of other brilliant and effective violin versions of pieces by great composers transcribed by Mischa Elman and Efrem Zimbalist; and I might mention specifically the latter's concert development of themes from Rimsky-Korsakoff's "Le Coq d'Or," published by G. Schirmer. Willy Burmeister, too, has contributed a large number of transcriptions to the repertoire, in particular the two well-known "Minuets" by Mozart and Beethoven. There are also very admirably finished and effective transcriptions of the older classic masters and of Hebrew folk melodies by Josef Achron, which have become very popular since Jascha Heifetz first introduced them in his concerts.

The literature of violin transcription is too vast to attempt any more extended mention of individual numbers. I shall content myself with mentioning a few pieces, transcriptions and originals, which represent individual preferences of my own among more recent publications.

Albert Spaulding, aside from his transcriptions—the Chopin "Valses" in B minor and G flat and Schubert's lovely "Hark, hark the lark"—has composed a theme with improvisations, "Etchings," which I consider one of the finest recent individual compositions written for the violin.

On the same high musical level I place the original "Souvenir Intime" and "Intermezzo Scherzoso" by Gustav Saenger.. The latter, too, has been very successful in making Scotch color violinistically convincing and musical in his original "Scotch Pastorale," which Mischa Elman in particular has included in his programs, and in his fine transcription of MacDowell's "Scotch Poem."

Like Albert Spalding, Cecil Burleigh has enriched violin literature with music of individual character, incontestably dramatic and original in its values. His noble Second Concerto, Op. 43, I personally consider, perhaps the outstanding creative achievement of its kind by an American composer. And his delightful "Plantation Sketches," Op. 36, which so happily have caught the spirit of southern negro melody and his intimate, sensitive "Nature Studies," Op. 23, are compositions whose acquaintance every serious student may profitably make.**

If it appear strange that I do not touch on the many admirable compositions by other American composers of distinction it is due to the fact that throughout my volume I have considered only music of which I can speak at first hand, music which I myself have studied or played.

All these compositions must be interpreted individually. It is wellnigh impossible to set down in detail exactly how they are to be conceived, and how they are to be played. The most satisfactory way for the student to arrive at a valid artistic interpretation would be for him to listen to some notable artist's playing of such a composition, and endeavor thoroughly to grasp and absorb the impression he receives. Then, modifying his impression according to his own individual artistic instinct, he may allow himself to be guided by the original version heard without, however lapsing into slavish imitation.

Since the matter of musical memory is intimately connected with the interpretation of the repertoire numbers which have been discussed in this volume, a few remarks may not be out of place and may appropriately conclude this last chapter of the book.

The whole question of musical memory, of the ability to "play by heart" when practicing or on the concert platform is one of the greatest moment with regard to interpretation. The faculty of being able to play or conduct from memory was one which attracted no little attention during the second half of the nineteenth century. With the exception of a few of the greatest virtuosos—artists like Liszt, Paganini, Ernst, Vieuxtemps, Bazzini, who usually performed their own works —playing from memory was not customary on the concert platform. I can recall in my youthful days having seen violinists of acknowledged reputation in the concert field standing in front of their music-desks when playing in concert, without any protest being raised either by the public or the press.

** In addition to the works mentioned, I take pleasure in calling attention to Mr. Burleigh's "Impromptu and Scherzo," "Six Pictures," Op. 30, and the "Scherzando Fantastique," Op 12. These and the compositions previously discussed are published by Carl Fischer, Inc.

The pianist Raoul Pugno,* well-known and highly appreciated in his day, always kept his music before him on the stand, with an assistant at his left hand to turn the page when he was playing with *orchestra* accompaniment. His *solo* numbers, however, he invariably played without notes. When I asked him why he doubted his memory in the first instance he said to me: "Once, when I was playing the Beethoven C minor Concerto at a *Concert-Colonne* in Paris, I suffered a lapse of memory. For several seconds, which seemed hours to me, my fingers strayed over the keyboard in a vain attempt to keep in touch with the orchestra, until at last I caught the thread I had lost. The recollection of the mental anguish I suffered on this occasion was so intense, that I never again could induce myself to play with orchestra without having my piano part in front of me."

It is true that the memory may be strengthened and fortified up to a certain point by practice. Yet from the moment when the nerves become a factor, as they do in public performance, all the training in the world may prove to be but a broken reed. Even under these conditions, however, we find individuals with exceptional memnotic gifts. I believe Richard Wagner was the first conductor to conduct his own works and Beethoven's Ninth Symphony without an orchestral score. He was followed by Hans Richter, Hans von Bülow and, more recently, by Toscanini and others. Yet before and after Wagner's time famous composers, among them Berlioz, Anton Rubinstein and later Tschaikovsky and Rimsky-Korsakoff did not venture to conduct without a score. And, with all due admiration for a good musical memory it is, in the last analysis, a talent of the second order.

The most incredible memnotic test ever recorded, perhaps, was that furnished by Mozart when in Rome with his father, in 1786, he heard Allegri's "Miserere"* sung from manu-

* He died in Moscow during a concert tour, some two years before the beginning of the World War.

* The Miserere" by Gregorio Allegri (1584-1652) is a favorite number on the programs of the New York Society of Musical Art and similar organizations, and the eighteenth century poet Heine, who heard it in Rome in Mozart's day, wrote of it: "The angel song of the 'Miserere' is the enchanting music which can thrill a human being; the purest harmony which through a thousand loops and bands of bitter and bitter-sweet tones, sighs for an ever renewed life."

script in the Sixtine Chapel during the Easter week, and was so moved by its beauty that after his request to be allowed to copy a work which seemed to him unique of its kind had been refused, he copied it from memory after one more hearing. This, of course, represents an exceptional feat; yet it was not Mozart's abnormal memory which made him one of the most inspired musicians of all time.

A good musical memory may be said to hide a certain danger where the musical student is concerned. Deceived by his easy grasp of the *notes* of the etudes and solo pieces of the repertoire, yet technically as well as musically uncertain, the immature student is apt to continue along the wrong path, intoxicated by his feats of memory, until an experienced hand guides him back to the right road, if it not be too late to do so.

Practicing without notes *before* the musical composition in question is absolutely within the student's grasp in every respect, is something I cannot too strongly advise against; since it does not only represent a loss of time but also encourages bad habits often impossible to break. Yet it is by no means my intention to discourage the student from cultivating musical memory to the best of his ability. On the contrary, memory can be trained. It is excellent practice to study every etude, every concert number *away* from the instrument, with the *eye alone*, until the composition in question, with every bit of shading, with every prescribed dynamic mark and sign, unrolls itself as a finished mental picture, complete in every detail.

I remember a distinguished financier of St. Petersburg, a man of large affairs who was an excellent amateur violinist, and was often asked to play in the *salons* he frequented. He could spare but little time for special memnotic practice, and so he hit upon an ingenious scheme of utilizing certain spare moments of his busy day which otherwise would have gone to waste. Every day, in his auto, as he drove from his home to his office and back again, he carried the composition which he happened to be preparing with him and studied it. Not in the shape of large sheets of music, but in miniature pages, some two and half by five inches, which fitted snugly in his pocket, and each of which, in a clear photographic reduction, was a facsimile of one of the full-size music pages of the composition. Thus he had the piece he was studying about him all the time, in a convenient "vest-pocket" form, and could take it out and improve whatever stray moments for study came his way. I mention the circumstance to show that usually "where there is a will there is a way."

Not until he has the complete mental picture of the work he wishes to play should the student attempt to play it from memory. If it is a piece with piano accompaniment I would advise that he have the actual music before his eyes when he tries to play it from memory for the first time, because the polyphony of the various voices, to which he is not accustomed, may otherwise mislead his ear. At the present time it would be out of the question for a young violinist to appear in public as a solo artist with a music-stand before him. It would disturb the general impression made by his playing, for there would be something distinctly school-boyish about it that would at once excite the distrust of the public.

This does not hold good of chamber-music, where all the participants are equally responsible, and a slip of memory on the part of one performer might embarrass the others and thus compromise the effect of the entire work. Playing from memory on the concert platform is an essential, but it should be attempted only after adequate preparation. And the matter of musical memory prompts a final reflection with which my remarks may appropriately conclude. Musical memory is *one* factor and *only one* of a number of factors involved in the *modus operandi* of musical interpretation. And with regard to interpretation it is not the undue stressing of any single factor, mechanical or emotional, which is productive of the finest and most genuinely satisfying results. It is the right adjustment and interplay of *all* the factors involved and their proper employ at the given moment which will allow the student to do the fullest justice to the work he seeks to interpret. And if he will bear in mind that the ideal interpretation of any composition depends on the ideal balance of the factors involved he will have made a stride in advance toward the solution of many a problem which may seem beyond his grasp.

A CATALOG OF SELECTED DOVER
BOOKS IN ALL FIELDS OF INTEREST

100 BEST-LOVED POEMS, Edited by Philip Smith. "The Passionate Shepherd to His Love," "Shall I compare thee to a summer's day?" "Death, be not proud," "The Raven," "The Road Not Taken," plus works by Blake, Wordsworth, Byron, Shelley, Keats, many others. 96pp. 5 3/16 x 8 1/4.   0-486-28553-7

100 SMALL HOUSES OF THE THIRTIES, Brown-Blodgett Company. Exterior photographs and floor plans for 100 charming structures. Illustrations of models accompanied by descriptions of interiors, color schemes, closet space, and other amenities. 200 illustrations. 112pp. 8 3/8 x 11.   0-486-44131-8

1000 TURN-OF-THE-CENTURY HOUSES: With Illustrations and Floor Plans, Herbert C. Chivers. Reproduced from a rare edition, this showcase of homes ranges from cottages and bungalows to sprawling mansions. Each house is meticulously illustrated and accompanied by complete floor plans. 256pp. 9 3/8 x 12 1/4.
                                                                          0-486-45596-3

101 GREAT AMERICAN POEMS, Edited by The American Poetry & Literacy Project. Rich treasury of verse from the 19th and 20th centuries includes works by Edgar Allan Poe, Robert Frost, Walt Whitman, Langston Hughes, Emily Dickinson, T. S. Eliot, other notables. 96pp. 5 3/16 x 8 1/4.   0-486-40158-8

101 GREAT SAMURAI PRINTS, Utagawa Kuniyoshi. Kuniyoshi was a master of the warrior woodblock print — and these 18th-century illustrations represent the pinnacle of his craft. Full-color portraits of renowned Japanese samurais pulse with movement, passion, and remarkably fine detail. 112pp. 8 3/8 x 11.   0-486-46523-3

ABC OF BALLET, Janet Grosser. Clearly worded, abundantly illustrated little guide defines basic ballet-related terms: arabesque, battement, pas de chat, relevé, sissonne, many others. Pronunciation guide included. Excellent primer. 48pp. 4 3/16 x 5 3/4.
                                                                          0-486-40871-X

ACCESSORIES OF DRESS: An Illustrated Encyclopedia, Katherine Lester and Bess Viola Oerke. Illustrations of hats, veils, wigs, cravats, shawls, shoes, gloves, and other accessories enhance an engaging commentary that reveals the humor and charm of the many-sided story of accessorized apparel. 644 figures and 59 plates. 608pp. 6 1/8 x 9 1/4.
                                                                          0-486-43378-1

ADVENTURES OF HUCKLEBERRY FINN, Mark Twain. Join Huck and Jim as their boyhood adventures along the Mississippi River lead them into a world of excitement, danger, and self-discovery. Humorous narrative, lyrical descriptions of the Mississippi valley, and memorable characters. 224pp. 5 3/16 x 8 1/4.   0-486-28061-6

ALICE STARMORE'S BOOK OF FAIR ISLE KNITTING, Alice Starmore. A noted designer from the region of Scotland's Fair Isle explores the history and techniques of this distinctive, stranded-color knitting style and provides copious illustrated instructions for 14 original knitwear designs. 208pp. 8 3/8 x 10 7/8.   0-486-47218-3

ALICE'S ADVENTURES IN WONDERLAND, Lewis Carroll. Beloved classic about a little girl lost in a topsy-turvy land and her encounters with the White Rabbit, March Hare, Mad Hatter, Cheshire Cat, and other delightfully improbable characters. 42 illustrations by Sir John Tenniel. 96pp. 5³⁄₁₆ x 8¼.   0-486-27543-4

AMERICA'S LIGHTHOUSES: An Illustrated History, Francis Ross Holland. Profusely illustrated fact-filled survey of American lighthouses since 1716. Over 200 stations — East, Gulf, and West coasts, Great Lakes, Hawaii, Alaska, Puerto Rico, the Virgin Islands, and the Mississippi and St. Lawrence Rivers. 240pp. 8 x 10¾.
0-486-25576-X

AN ENCYCLOPEDIA OF THE VIOLIN, Alberto Bachmann. Translated by Frederick H. Martens. Introduction by Eugene Ysaye. First published in 1925, this renowned reference remains unsurpassed as a source of essential information, from construction and evolution to repertoire and technique. Includes a glossary and 73 illustrations. 496pp. 6⅛ x 9¼.   0-486-46618-3

ANIMALS: 1,419 Copyright-Free Illustrations of Mammals, Birds, Fish, Insects, etc., Selected by Jim Harter. Selected for its visual impact and ease of use, this outstanding collection of wood engravings presents over 1,000 species of animals in extremely lifelike poses. Includes mammals, birds, reptiles, amphibians, fish, insects, and other invertebrates. 284pp. 9 x 12.   0-486-23766-4

THE ANNALS, Tacitus. Translated by Alfred John Church and William Jackson Brodribb. This vital chronicle of Imperial Rome, written by the era's great historian, spans A.D. 14-68 and paints incisive psychological portraits of major figures, from Tiberius to Nero. 416pp. 5³⁄₁₆ x 8¼.   0-486-45236-0

ANTIGONE, Sophocles. Filled with passionate speeches and sensitive probing of moral and philosophical issues, this powerful and often-performed Greek drama reveals the grim fate that befalls the children of Oedipus. Footnotes. 64pp. 5³⁄₁₆ x 8 ¼.   0-486-27804-2

ART DECO DECORATIVE PATTERNS IN FULL COLOR, Christian Stoll. Reprinted from a rare 1910 portfolio, 160 sensuous and exotic images depict a breathtaking array of florals, geometrics, and abstracts — all elegant in their stark simplicity. 64pp. 8⅜ x 11.   0-486-44862-2

THE ARTHUR RACKHAM TREASURY: 86 Full-Color Illustrations, Arthur Rackham. Selected and Edited by Jeff A. Menges. A stunning treasury of 86 full-page plates span the famed English artist's career, from *Rip Van Winkle* (1905) to masterworks such as *Undine, A Midsummer Night's Dream,* and *Wind in the Willows* (1939). 96pp. 8⅜ x 11.
0-486-44685-9

THE AUTHENTIC GILBERT & SULLIVAN SONGBOOK, W. S. Gilbert and A. S. Sullivan. The most comprehensive collection available, this songbook includes selections from every one of Gilbert and Sullivan's light operas. Ninety-two numbers are presented uncut and unedited, and in their original keys. 410pp. 9 x 12.
0-486-23482-7

THE AWAKENING, Kate Chopin. First published in 1899, this controversial novel of a New Orleans wife's search for love outside a stifling marriage shocked readers. Today, it remains a first-rate narrative with superb characterization. New introductory Note. 128pp. 5³⁄₁₆ x 8¼.   0-486-27786-0

BASIC DRAWING, Louis Priscilla. Beginning with perspective, this commonsense manual progresses to the figure in movement, light and shade, anatomy, drapery, composition, trees and landscape, and outdoor sketching. Black-and-white illustrations throughout. 128pp. 8⅜ x 11.   0-486-45815-6

THE BATTLES THAT CHANGED HISTORY, Fletcher Pratt. Historian profiles 16 crucial conflicts, ancient to modern, that changed the course of Western civilization. Gripping accounts of battles led by Alexander the Great, Joan of Arc, Ulysses S. Grant, other commanders. 27 maps. 352pp. 5⅜ x 8½. 0-486-41129-X

BEETHOVEN'S LETTERS, Ludwig van Beethoven. Edited by Dr. A. C. Kalischer. Features 457 letters to fellow musicians, friends, greats, patrons, and literary men. Reveals musical thoughts, quirks of personality, insights, and daily events. Includes 15 plates. 410pp. 5⅜ x 8½. 0-486-22769-3

BERNICE BOBS HER HAIR AND OTHER STORIES, F. Scott Fitzgerald. This brilliant anthology includes 6 of Fitzgerald's most popular stories: "The Diamond as Big as the Ritz," the title tale, "The Offshore Pirate," "The Ice Palace," "The Jelly Bean," and "May Day." 176pp. 5⅜ x 8½. 0-486-47049-0

BESLER'S BOOK OF FLOWERS AND PLANTS: 73 Full-Color Plates from Hortus Eystettensis, 1613, Basilius Besler. Here is a selection of magnificent plates from the *Hortus Eystettensis,* which vividly illustrated and identified the plants, flowers, and trees that thrived in the legendary German garden at Eichstätt. 80pp. 8⅜ x 11. 0-486-46005-3

THE BOOK OF KELLS, Edited by Blanche Cirker. Painstakingly reproduced from a rare facsimile edition, this volume contains full-page decorations, portraits, illustrations, plus a sampling of textual leaves with exquisite calligraphy and ornamentation. 32 full-color illustrations. 32pp. 9⅜ x 12¼. 0-486-24345-1

THE BOOK OF THE CROSSBOW: With an Additional Section on Catapults and Other Siege Engines, Ralph Payne-Gallwey. Fascinating study traces history and use of crossbow as military and sporting weapon, from Middle Ages to modern times. Also covers related weapons: balistas, catapults, Turkish bows, more. Over 240 illustrations. 400pp. 7¼ x 10⅛. 0-486-28720-3

THE BUNGALOW BOOK: Floor Plans and Photos of 112 Houses, 1910, Henry L. Wilson. Here are 112 of the most popular and economic blueprints of the early 20th century — plus an illustration or photograph of each completed house. A wonderful time capsule that still offers a wealth of valuable insights. 160pp. 8⅜ x 11. 0-486-45104-6

THE CALL OF THE WILD, Jack London. A classic novel of adventure, drawn from London's own experiences as a Klondike adventurer, relating the story of a heroic dog caught in the brutal life of the Alaska Gold Rush. Note. 64pp. 5³⁄₁₆ x 8¼. 0-486-26472-6

CANDIDE, Voltaire. Edited by Francois-Marie Arouet. One of the world's great satires since its first publication in 1759. Witty, caustic skewering of romance, science, philosophy, religion, government — nearly all human ideals and institutions. 112pp. 5³⁄₁₆ x 8¼. 0-486-26689-3

CELEBRATED IN THEIR TIME: Photographic Portraits from the George Grantham Bain Collection, Edited by Amy Pastan. With an Introduction by Michael Carlebach. Remarkable portrait gallery features 112 rare images of Albert Einstein, Charlie Chaplin, the Wright Brothers, Henry Ford, and other luminaries from the worlds of politics, art, entertainment, and industry. 128pp. 8⅜ x 11. 0-486-46754-6

CHARIOTS FOR APOLLO: The NASA History of Manned Lunar Spacecraft to 1969, Courtney G. Brooks, James M. Grimwood, and Loyd S. Swenson, Jr. This illustrated history by a trio of experts is the definitive reference on the Apollo spacecraft and lunar modules. It traces the vehicles' design, development, and operation in space. More than 100 photographs and illustrations. 576pp. 6¾ x 9¼. 0-486-46756-2

A CHRISTMAS CAROL, Charles Dickens. This engrossing tale relates Ebenezer Scrooge's ghostly journeys through Christmases past, present, and future and his ultimate transformation from a harsh and grasping old miser to a charitable and compassionate human being. 80pp. 5¾₆ x 8¼. 0-486-26865-9

COMMON SENSE, Thomas Paine. First published in January of 1776, this highly influential landmark document clearly and persuasively argued for American separation from Great Britain and paved the way for the Declaration of Independence. 64pp. 5¾₆ x 8¼. 0-486-29602-4

THE COMPLETE SHORT STORIES OF OSCAR WILDE, Oscar Wilde. Complete texts of "The Happy Prince and Other Tales," "A House of Pomegranates," "Lord Arthur Savile's Crime and Other Stories," "Poems in Prose," and "The Portrait of Mr. W. H." 208pp. 5¾₆ x 8¼. 0-486-45216-6

COMPLETE SONNETS, William Shakespeare. Over 150 exquisite poems deal with love, friendship, the tyranny of time, beauty's evanescence, death, and other themes in language of remarkable power, precision, and beauty. Glossary of archaic terms. 80pp. 5¾₆ x 8¼. 0-486-26686-9

THE COUNT OF MONTE CRISTO: Abridged Edition, Alexandre Dumas. Falsely accused of treason, Edmond Dantès is imprisoned in the bleak Chateau d'If. After a hair-raising escape, he launches an elaborate plot to extract a bitter revenge against those who betrayed him. 448pp. 5¾₆ x 8¼. 0-486-45643-9

CRAFTSMAN BUNGALOWS: Designs from the Pacific Northwest, Yoho & Merritt. This reprint of a rare catalog, showcasing the charming simplicity and cozy style of Craftsman bungalows, is filled with photos of completed homes, plus floor plans and estimated costs. An indispensable resource for architects, historians, and illustrators. 112pp. 10 x 7. 0-486-46875-5

CRAFTSMAN BUNGALOWS: 59 Homes from "The Craftsman," Edited by Gustav Stickley. Best and most attractive designs from Arts and Crafts Movement publication — 1903–1916 — includes sketches, photographs of homes, floor plans, descriptive text. 128pp. 8¼ x 11. 0-486-25829-7

CRIME AND PUNISHMENT, Fyodor Dostoyevsky. Translated by Constance Garnett. Supreme masterpiece tells the story of Raskolnikov, a student tormented by his own thoughts after he murders an old woman. Overwhelmed by guilt and terror, he confesses and goes to prison. 480pp. 5¾₆ x 8¼. 0-486-41587-2

THE DECLARATION OF INDEPENDENCE AND OTHER GREAT DOCUMENTS OF AMERICAN HISTORY: 1775-1865, Edited by John Grafton. Thirteen compelling and influential documents: Henry's "Give Me Liberty or Give Me Death," Declaration of Independence, The Constitution, Washington's First Inaugural Address, The Monroe Doctrine, The Emancipation Proclamation, Gettysburg Address, more. 64pp. 5¾₆ x 8¼. 0-486-41124-9

THE DESERT AND THE SOWN: Travels in Palestine and Syria, Gertrude Bell. "The female Lawrence of Arabia," Gertrude Bell wrote captivating, perceptive accounts of her travels in the Middle East. This intriguing narrative, accompanied by 160 photos, traces her 1905 sojourn in Lebanon, Syria, and Palestine. 368pp. 5⅜ x 8½. 0-486-46876-3

A DOLL'S HOUSE, Henrik Ibsen. Ibsen's best-known play displays his genius for realistic prose drama. An expression of women's rights, the play climaxes when the central character, Nora, rejects a smothering marriage and life in "a doll's house." 80pp. 5¾₆ x 8¼. 0-486-27062-9

Browse over 9,000 books at www.doverpublications.com

DOOMED SHIPS: Great Ocean Liner Disasters, William H. Miller, Jr. Nearly 200 photographs, many from private collections, highlight tales of some of the vessels whose pleasure cruises ended in catastrophe: the *Morro Castle, Normandie, Andrea Doria, Europa,* and many others. 128pp. 8⅛ x 11¾. 0-486-45366-9

THE DORÉ BIBLE ILLUSTRATIONS, Gustave Doré. Detailed plates from the Bible: the Creation scenes, Adam and Eve, horrifying visions of the Flood, the battle sequences with their monumental crowds, depictions of the life of Jesus, 241 plates in all. 241pp. 9 x 12. 0-486-23004-X

DRAWING DRAPERY FROM HEAD TO TOE, Cliff Young. Expert guidance on how to draw shirts, pants, skirts, gloves, hats, and coats on the human figure, including folds in relation to the body, pull and crush, action folds, creases, more. Over 200 drawings. 48pp. 8¼ x 11. 0-486-45591-2

DUBLINERS, James Joyce. A fine and accessible introduction to the work of one of the 20th century's most influential writers, this collection features 15 tales, including a masterpiece of the short-story genre, "The Dead." 160pp. 5³⁄₁₆ x 8¼.

0-486-26870-5

EASY-TO-MAKE POP-UPS, Joan Irvine. Illustrated by Barbara Reid. Dozens of wonderful ideas for three-dimensional paper fun — from holiday greeting cards with moving parts to a pop-up menagerie. Easy-to-follow, illustrated instructions for more than 30 projects. 299 black-and-white illustrations. 96pp. 8⅜ x 11.

0-486-44622-0

EASY-TO-MAKE STORYBOOK DOLLS: A "Novel" Approach to Cloth Dollmaking, Sherralyn St. Clair. Favorite fictional characters come alive in this unique beginner's dollmaking guide. Includes patterns for Pollyanna, Dorothy from *The Wonderful Wizard of Oz,* Mary of *The Secret Garden,* plus easy-to-follow instructions, 263 black-and-white illustrations, and an 8-page color insert. 112pp. 8¼ x 11. 0-486-47360-0

EINSTEIN'S ESSAYS IN SCIENCE, Albert Einstein. Speeches and essays in accessible, everyday language profile influential physicists such as Niels Bohr and Isaac Newton. They also explore areas of physics to which the author made major contributions. 128pp. 5 x 8. 0-486-47011-3

EL DORADO: Further Adventures of the Scarlet Pimpernel, Baroness Orczy. A popular sequel to *The Scarlet Pimpernel,* this suspenseful story recounts the Pimpernel's attempts to rescue the Dauphin from imprisonment during the French Revolution. An irresistible blend of intrigue, period detail, and vibrant characterizations. 352pp. 5³⁄₁₆ x 8¼. 0-486-44026-5

ELEGANT SMALL HOMES OF THE TWENTIES: 99 Designs from a Competition, Chicago Tribune. Nearly 100 designs for five- and six-room houses feature New England and Southern colonials, Normandy cottages, stately Italianate dwellings, and other fascinating snapshots of American domestic architecture of the 1920s. 112pp. 9 x 12. 0-486-46910-7

THE ELEMENTS OF STYLE: The Original Edition, William Strunk, Jr. This is the book that generations of writers have relied upon for timeless advice on grammar, diction, syntax, and other essentials. In concise terms, it identifies the principal requirements of proper style and common errors. 64pp. 5⅜ x 8½. 0-486-44798-7

THE ELUSIVE PIMPERNEL, Baroness Orczy. Robespierre's revolutionaries find their wicked schemes thwarted by the heroic Pimpernel — Sir Percival Blakeney. In this thrilling sequel, Chauvelin devises a plot to eliminate the Pimpernel and his wife. 272pp. 5³⁄₁₆ x 8¼. 0-486-45464-9

Browse over 9,000 books at www.doverpublications.com

AN ENCYCLOPEDIA OF BATTLES: Accounts of Over 1,560 Battles from 1479 B.C. to the Present, David Eggenberger. Essential details of every major battle in recorded history from the first battle of Megiddo in 1479 B.C. to Grenada in 1984. List of battle maps. 99 illustrations. 544pp. 6½ x 9¼. 0-486-24913-1

ENCYCLOPEDIA OF EMBROIDERY STITCHES, INCLUDING CREWEL, Marion Nichols. Precise explanations and instructions, clearly illustrated, on how to work chain, back, cross, knotted, woven stitches, and many more — 178 in all, including Cable Outline, Whipped Satin, and Eyelet Buttonhole. Over 1400 illustrations. 219pp. 8⅜ x 11¼. 0-486-22929-7

ENTER JEEVES: 15 Early Stories, P. G. Wodehouse. Splendid collection contains first 8 stories featuring Bertie Wooster, the deliciously dim aristocrat and Jeeves, his brainy, imperturbable manservant. Also, the complete Reggie Pepper (Bertie's prototype) series. 288pp. 5⅜ x 8½. 0-486-29717-9

ERIC SLOANE'S AMERICA: Paintings in Oil, Michael Wigley. With a Foreword by Mimi Sloane. Eric Sloane's evocative oils of America's landscape and material culture shimmer with immense historical and nostalgic appeal. This original hardcover collection gathers nearly a hundred of his finest paintings, with subjects ranging from New England to the American Southwest. 128pp. 10⅝ x 9. 0-486-46525-X

ETHAN FROME, Edith Wharton. Classic story of wasted lives, set against a bleak New England background. Superbly delineated characters in a hauntingly grim tale of thwarted love. Considered by many to be Wharton's masterpiece. 96pp. 5³⁄₁₆ x 8 ¼. 0-486-26690-7

THE EVERLASTING MAN, G. K. Chesterton. Chesterton's view of Christianity — as a blend of philosophy and mythology, satisfying intellect and spirit — applies to his brilliant book, which appeals to readers' heads as well as their hearts. 288pp. 5⅜ x 8½. 0-486-46036-3

THE FIELD AND FOREST HANDY BOOK, Daniel Beard. Written by a co-founder of the Boy Scouts, this appealing guide offers illustrated instructions for building kites, birdhouses, boats, igloos, and other fun projects, plus numerous helpful tips for campers. 448pp. 5³⁄₁₆ x 8¼. 0-486-46191-2

FINDING YOUR WAY WITHOUT MAP OR COMPASS, Harold Gatty. Useful, instructive manual shows would-be explorers, hikers, bikers, scouts, sailors, and survivalists how to find their way outdoors by observing animals, weather patterns, shifting sands, and other elements of nature. 288pp. 5⅜ x 8½. 0-486-40613-X

FIRST FRENCH READER: A Beginner's Dual-Language Book, Edited and Translated by Stanley Appelbaum. This anthology introduces 50 legendary writers — Voltaire, Balzac, Baudelaire, Proust, more — through passages from *The Red and the Black, Les Misérables, Madame Bovary,* and other classics. Original French text plus English translation on facing pages. 240pp. 5⅜ x 8½. 0-486-46178-5

FIRST GERMAN READER: A Beginner's Dual-Language Book, Edited by Harry Steinhauer. Specially chosen for their power to evoke German life and culture, these short, simple readings include poems, stories, essays, and anecdotes by Goethe, Hesse, Heine, Schiller, and others. 224pp. 5⅜ x 8½. 0-486-46179-3

FIRST SPANISH READER: A Beginner's Dual-Language Book, Angel Flores. Delightful stories, other material based on works of Don Juan Manuel, Luis Taboada, Ricardo Palma, other noted writers. Complete faithful English translations on facing pages. Exercises. 176pp. 5⅜ x 8½. 0-486-25810-6

FIVE ACRES AND INDEPENDENCE, Maurice G. Kains. Great back-to-the-land classic explains basics of self-sufficient farming. The one book to get. 95 illustrations. 397pp. 5⅜ x 8½. 0-486-20974-1

FLAGG'S SMALL HOUSES: Their Economic Design and Construction, 1922, Ernest Flagg. Although most famous for his skyscrapers, Flagg was also a proponent of the well-designed single-family dwelling. His classic treatise features innovations that save space, materials, and cost. 526 illustrations. 160pp. 9⅜ x 12¼. 0-486-45197-6

FLATLAND: A Romance of Many Dimensions, Edwin A. Abbott. Classic of science (and mathematical) fiction — charmingly illustrated by the author — describes the adventures of A. Square, a resident of Flatland, in Spaceland (three dimensions), Lineland (one dimension), and Pointland (no dimensions). 96pp. 5 3/16 x 8¼. 0-486-27263-X

FRANKENSTEIN, Mary Shelley. The story of Victor Frankenstein's monstrous creation and the havoc it caused has enthralled generations of readers and inspired countless writers of horror and suspense. With the author's own 1831 introduction. 176pp. 5 3/16 x 8¼. 0-486-28211-2

THE GARGOYLE BOOK: 572 Examples from Gothic Architecture, Lester Burbank Bridaham. Dispelling the conventional wisdom that French Gothic architectural flourishes were born of despair or gloom, Bridaham reveals the whimsical nature of these creations and the ingenious artisans who made them. 572 illustrations. 224pp. 8⅜ x 11. 0-486-44754-5

THE GIFT OF THE MAGI AND OTHER SHORT STORIES, O. Henry. Sixteen captivating stories by one of America's most popular storytellers. Included are such classics as "The Gift of the Magi," "The Last Leaf," and "The Ransom of Red Chief." Publisher's Note. 96pp. 5 3/16 x 8¼. 0-486-27061-0

THE GOETHE TREASURY: Selected Prose and Poetry, Johann Wolfgang von Goethe. Edited, Selected, and with an Introduction by Thomas Mann. In addition to his lyric poetry, Goethe wrote travel sketches, autobiographical studies, essays, letters, and proverbs in rhyme and prose. This collection presents outstanding examples from each genre. 368pp. 5⅜ x 8½. 0-486-44780-4

GREAT EXPECTATIONS, Charles Dickens. Orphaned Pip is apprenticed to the dirty work of the forge but dreams of becoming a gentleman — and one day finds himself in possession of "great expectations." Dickens' finest novel. 400pp. 5 3/16 x 8¼. 0-486-41586-4

GREAT WRITERS ON THE ART OF FICTION: From Mark Twain to Joyce Carol Oates, Edited by James Daley. An indispensable source of advice and inspiration, this anthology features essays by Henry James, Kate Chopin, Willa Cather, Sinclair Lewis, Jack London, Raymond Chandler, Raymond Carver, Eudora Welty, and Kurt Vonnegut, Jr. 192pp. 5⅜ x 8½. 0-486-45128-3

HAMLET, William Shakespeare. The quintessential Shakespearean tragedy, whose highly charged confrontations and anguished soliloquies probe depths of human feeling rarely sounded in any art. Reprinted from an authoritative British edition complete with illuminating footnotes. 128pp. 5 3/16 x 8¼. 0-486-27278-8

THE HAUNTED HOUSE, Charles Dickens. A Yuletide gathering in an eerie country retreat provides the backdrop for Dickens and his friends — including Elizabeth Gaskell and Wilkie Collins — who take turns spinning supernatural yarns. 144pp. 5⅜ x 8½. 0-486-46309-5

Browse over 9,000 books at www.doverpublications.com

HEART OF DARKNESS, Joseph Conrad. Dark allegory of a journey up the Congo River and the narrator's encounter with the mysterious Mr. Kurtz. Masterly blend of adventure, character study, psychological penetration. For many, Conrad's finest, most enigmatic story. 80pp. 5³⁄₁₆ x 8¼.   0-486-26464-5

HENSON AT THE NORTH POLE, Matthew A. Henson. This thrilling memoir by the heroic African-American who was Peary's companion through two decades of Arctic exploration recounts a tale of danger, courage, and determination. "Fascinating and exciting." — *Commonweal.* 128pp. 5⅜ x 8½.   0-486-45472-X

HISTORIC COSTUMES AND HOW TO MAKE THEM, Mary Fernald and E. Shenton. Practical, informative guidebook shows how to create everything from short tunics worn by Saxon men in the fifth century to a lady's bustle dress of the late 1800s. 81 illustrations. 176pp. 5⅜ x 8½.   0-486-44906-8

THE HOUND OF THE BASKERVILLES, Arthur Conan Doyle. A deadly curse in the form of a legendary ferocious beast continues to claim its victims from the Baskerville family until Holmes and Watson intervene. Often called the best detective story ever written. 128pp. 5³⁄₁₆ x 8¼.   0-486-28214-7

THE HOUSE BEHIND THE CEDARS, Charles W. Chesnutt. Originally published in 1900, this groundbreaking novel by a distinguished African-American author recounts the drama of a brother and sister who "pass for white" during the dangerous days of Reconstruction. 208pp. 5⅜ x 8½.   0-486-46144-0

THE HUMAN FIGURE IN MOTION, Eadweard Muybridge. The 4,789 photographs in this definitive selection show the human figure — models almost all undraped — engaged in over 160 different types of action: running, climbing stairs, etc. 390pp. 7⅞ x 10⅝.   0-486-20204-6

THE IMPORTANCE OF BEING EARNEST, Oscar Wilde. Wilde's witty and buoyant comedy of manners, filled with some of literature's most famous epigrams, reprinted from an authoritative British edition. Considered Wilde's most perfect work. 64pp. 5³⁄₁₆ x 8¼.   0-486-26478-5

THE INFERNO, Dante Alighieri. Translated and with notes by Henry Wadsworth Longfellow. The first stop on Dante's famous journey from Hell to Purgatory to Paradise, this 14th-century allegorical poem blends vivid and shocking imagery with graceful lyricism. Translated by the beloved 19th-century poet, Henry Wadsworth Longfellow. 256pp. 5³⁄₁₆ x 8¼.   0-486-44288-8

JANE EYRE, Charlotte Brontë. Written in 1847, *Jane Eyre* tells the tale of an orphan girl's progress from the custody of cruel relatives to an oppressive boarding school and its culmination in a troubled career as a governess. 448pp. 5³⁄₁₆ x 8¼.
                    0-486-42449-9

JAPANESE WOODBLOCK FLOWER PRINTS, Tanigami Kônan. Extraordinary collection of Japanese woodblock prints by a well-known artist features 120 plates in brilliant color. Realistic images from a rare edition include daffodils, tulips, and other familiar and unusual flowers. 128pp. 11 x 8¼.   0-486-46442-3

JEWELRY MAKING AND DESIGN, Augustus F. Rose and Antonio Cirino. Professional secrets of jewelry making are revealed in a thorough, practical guide. Over 200 illustrations. 306pp. 5⅜ x 8½.   0-486-21750-7

JULIUS CAESAR, William Shakespeare. Great tragedy based on Plutarch's account of the lives of Brutus, Julius Caesar and Mark Antony. Evil plotting, ringing oratory, high tragedy with Shakespeare's incomparable insight, dramatic power. Explanatory footnotes. 96pp. 5³⁄₁₆ x 8¼.   0-486-26876-4

THE JUNGLE, Upton Sinclair. 1906 bestseller shockingly reveals intolerable labor practices and working conditions in the Chicago stockyards as it tells the grim story of a Slavic family that emigrates to America full of optimism but soon faces despair. 320pp. 5³⁄₁₆ x 8¼. 0-486-41923-1

THE KINGDOM OF GOD IS WITHIN YOU, Leo Tolstoy. The soul-searching book that inspired Gandhi to embrace the concept of passive resistance, Tolstoy's 1894 polemic clearly outlines a radical, well-reasoned revision of traditional Christian thinking. 352pp. 5³⁄₁₆ x 8¼. 0-486-45138-0

THE LADY OR THE TIGER?: and Other Logic Puzzles, Raymond M. Smullyan. Created by a renowned puzzle master, these whimsically themed challenges involve paradoxes about probability, time, and change; metapuzzles; and self-referentiality. Nineteen chapters advance in difficulty from relatively simple to highly complex. 1982 edition. 240pp. 5⅜ x 8½. 0-486-47027-X

LEAVES OF GRASS: The Original 1855 Edition, Walt Whitman. Whitman's immortal collection includes some of the greatest poems of modern times, including his masterpiece, "Song of Myself." Shattering standard conventions, it stands as an unabashed celebration of body and nature. 128pp. 5³⁄₁₆ x 8¼. 0-486-45676-5

LES MISÉRABLES, Victor Hugo. Translated by Charles E. Wilbour. Abridged by James K. Robinson. A convict's heroic struggle for justice and redemption plays out against a fiery backdrop of the Napoleonic wars. This edition features the excellent original translation and a sensitive abridgment. 304pp. 6⅛ x 9¼. 0-486-45789-3

LILITH: A Romance, George MacDonald. In this novel by the father of fantasy literature, a man travels through time to meet Adam and Eve and to explore humanity's fall from grace and ultimate redemption. 240pp. 5⅜ x 8½. 0-486-46818-6

THE LOST LANGUAGE OF SYMBOLISM, Harold Bayley. This remarkable book reveals the hidden meaning behind familiar images and words, from the origins of Santa Claus to the fleur-de-lys, drawing from mythology, folklore, religious texts, and fairy tales. 1,418 illustrations. 784pp. 5⅜ x 8½. 0-486-44787-1

MACBETH, William Shakespeare. A Scottish nobleman murders the king in order to succeed to the throne. Tortured by his conscience and fearful of discovery, he becomes tangled in a web of treachery and deceit that ultimately spells his doom. 96pp. 5³⁄₁₆ x 8¼. 0-486-27802-6

MAKING AUTHENTIC CRAFTSMAN FURNITURE: Instructions and Plans for 62 Projects, Gustav Stickley. Make authentic reproductions of handsome, functional, durable furniture: tables, chairs, wall cabinets, desks, a hall tree, and more. Construction plans with drawings, schematics, dimensions, and lumber specs reprinted from 1900s The Craftsman magazine. 128pp. 8⅛ x 11. 0-486-25000-8

MATHEMATICS FOR THE NONMATHEMATICIAN, Morris Kline. Erudite and entertaining overview follows development of mathematics from ancient Greeks to present. Topics include logic and mathematics, the fundamental concept, differential calculus, probability theory, much more. Exercises and problems. 641pp. 5⅜ x 8½. 0-486-24823-2

MEMOIRS OF AN ARABIAN PRINCESS FROM ZANZIBAR, Emily Ruete. This 19th-century autobiography offers a rare inside look at the society surrounding a sultan's palace. A real-life princess in exile recalls her vanished world of harems, slave trading, and court intrigues. 288pp. 5⅜ x 8½. 0-486-47121-7